True Hollywood Noir

Filmland Mysteries and Murders

by Dina Di Mambro

Di Mambro, Dina, *True Hollywood Noir: Filmland Mysteries and Murders*/Dina Di Mambro

Copyright © 2013 Dina Di Mambro

All rights reserved.

ISBN-10: 1492338850

ISBN-13: 9781492338857 (**Classichollywoodbios.com Publications**)

Library of Congress Control Number: 2011944541

CreateSpace Independent Publishing Platform

North Charleston, South Carolina

Front Cover: Natalie Wood Publicity Portrait/Silver Screen Cinema Collection. Gangster Mickey Cohen in 1949 (Photo by Ed Clark//Time Life Pictures/Getty Images). Gig Young Publicity Portrait/Silver Screen Cinema Collection. George Reeves as Superman © Motion Pictures for Television Inc./Photofest. Lana Turner 1940s Portrait/Photofest. *Hogan's Heroes* 1965-1971, shown Bob Crane at Lt. Robert Hogan, CBS/Photofest © CBS. A portrait of Jean Harlow by Clarence Bull made on December 16, 1930/Photofest. .

Back Cover: Author Photo/Tammy Warnock/True Blue Photography. www.truebluephotography.com – Hair and Makeup: Ali Robles

As Dina-Marie Kulzer, Dina Di Mambro authored *Television Series Regulars of the Fifties and Sixties in Interview* © 1992, 2012. McFarland & Company, Inc. Publishers. www.mcfarland.com

Author Websites

www.classichollywoodbios.com

http://www.classichollywoodbios.com/truehollywoodnoir.htm

To my generous, overprotective father Vittorio Di Mambro and my beautiful, sassy mother Sharon Neal Di Mambro. And to their mothers, Maria Libera, who had a great desire to learn to read, and Eileen, where my love of writing came from.

and

To the individuals featured in this book who are no longer with us—particularly those who met with untimely tragic ends. May your spirits find peace and know that you are still remembered, loved, and admired not only in the memory of friends and family left behind but those whose lives you've touched through your talent and work that remain timeless.

Pictured: Dina Di Mambro, Author

A special thank you to Tammy Waronek of www.truebluephotography.com for being my personal "George Hurrell." I always dreamed of having a photograph like this. You are nothing less than a magician. Make Up and Hair: Ali Robles

Acknowledgements

My heartfelt thanks to Jim Smith for his generosity of information in the Johnny Stompanato/Lana Turner chapter and for, in essence, providing the entire Mickey Cohen chapter (as well as treasured photographs). I would have had to give him a co-authorship in this book if he had helped me with any additional chapters, and he could have. (The man knows absolutely *everyone.*) Jim doesn't generally talk to writers, and I am so thankful that he shared his memories with me. It is my hope that future authors will cite and take into account Smith's first-hand memories rather than the fiction that has been perpetuated for so many years. You have my eternal gratitude, Jim.

To Sara, John, and Lilly Ibrahim, thank you for your hospitality and providing cherished family photographs. To John Ibrahim (Stompanato), Erlene Wille, Skye Aubrey, and "stand-up guy" John-John Solari, for sharing your memories in candid interviews. Judy Shaw, thank you for acting as my editor. I greatly appreciate your help. Chris Ragon, I am so grateful for your assistance with the photographs. To Ted James at www.celebritycollectables.com, thank you for providing official documents such as wills, coroners' inquests, and autopsy reports. And thanks to my long-suffering husband Carl Kulzer for putting up with these same documents being strewn about the kitchen table (not very appetizing) and being the very first set of eyes, besides my own, to read my chapters. Carl's sister Karen, her husband John, and their son Kevin Kula have always been very caring…thank you.

And on a personal note, special thanks to my family who provided inspiration and support, in particular my parents, Sharon and Vittorio Di

Mambro (Daddy, I used the family name on this one!), my brother John Di Mambro, my Uncle Dean Neal (who is always so encouraging and sweet to me) and my *Zia* (Aunt) Anna Di Mambro. Anna's granddaughters Emma Thompson and Nicole Thompson are gifted, young writers…the next generation. Carry the torch, girls; I'm getting a little tired. And to Shandora Roberts Scanlon, "Shani," (my little girl, not biologically but in my heart) who has two beautiful young daughters, Mya and Madelyn, of her own. They remind me so much of you. I am proud of the young woman you have become. Other children of my heart now grown, Nicolas Canale and Stephanie Canale Tambe…I'm happy your parents let me borrow you and return you to them thoroughly spoiled. You are very special to me.

And a special thanks to my friends, you know who you are. There are certain friends who I forced to drop everything and read first drafts of some of my chapters. They were among my first sets of eyes. Other friends encouraged me and convinced me I wouldn't bore my readers into a coma. Hope you guys were right. Thank you to my supportive friend Marilyn Morton, a wonderful singer, who was once known as "Sami," when she sang in Las Vegas with the Norman Brown Sextet. Thanks to Xavier and Gabrielle Canale and Robert and Eve Brittany. I cherish your friendship. Eve is my most enthusiastic champion. And my sincere thanks to my new, dear friends whom I met at the Turner Classic Movies Film Festival, they have their reasons for remaining anonymous. You two gentlemen have provided so much support and love. You are the happiest couple I know. I treasure you both. Thank you for believing in me. BCD your friendship means a great deal to me. Aunt Connie ("Mariuccia") and Uncle Mario Di Mambro thank you for buying me my first movie books. Look what you started! Love you both so much. And thanks to my Aunt Donna Neal Shelley for your continued interest in my writing. Tally Haugen, my fellow classic film enthusiast, also helped clean up some ancient, grainy images…thank you.

And to my little muse, my gorgeous cat Sunny, who sat perched above me many a night as I wrote, supervising me when not engaging in more interesting activities, such as tearing post-it notes, chasing pens, flipping index cards and knocking books over.

Table of Contents

Introduction

Film Noir—translated from French as "black film"—is a genre that encompasses the elements of highly charged sexuality with cynical male characters, femme fatales, and moral ambiguity. Or as author Charles Pappas described it, "the language of losers…always about the same things: sex, violence, and money." Swirling cigarette smoke; high balls on ice; murky, rain-soaked nights; ill-fated plots between gangsters and grifters; and hard-boiled detectives and duplicitous gorgeous women with an agenda were all readily evident in *The Maltese Falcon* (1941), *Double Indemnity, Laura, and The Woman in the Window* (1944), *Gilda,* and *The Postman Always Rings Twice* (1946) through to Orson Welles's *Touch of Evil* (1958).

The crime dramas of the war years and the *film noirs* of the post war period were the antidotes to the happy-go-lucky musicals and screwball comedies that had previously dominated the screen. Following World War II and going forward into the cold war era, audiences had experienced more, and their tastes deepened and matured.

The actors and directors who created these stylish black and white masterpieces with the artistic use of shadows and light and tilted camera angles to convey mood and emotion lived existences that made many of the plots of their films pale in comparison. Welcome to the true Hollywood Noir and the stories of the players behind the scenes. From 1922 until 2001, this book explores some of the most fascinating scandals, mysteries, and murders in Filmland history. The chapters in this book explore the various theories in each case…it is up to the reader to make up his or her mind.

The west coast mob, city corruption, and Hollywood mysteries were often intertwined. This is a common thread through much of this book and is expanded upon in the Mickey Cohen chapter. Many of the plots of the *noir* films were taken from actual happenings in the underworld, which the Mickey Cohen chapter reveals.

Could it have been the plots they played out during the day at the studio that contributed to the sense of drama and roller coaster emotions in their private lives? While most of the actors featured in this book met with untimely tragic deaths or notorious misfortune that colored the remainder of their lives, the talent of these highly creative individuals and the legacy they've left us continues to give them a special kind of immortality. Their work lives on…as flickering images on a screen…great talents never to be forgotten.

CHAPTER 1

William Desmond Taylor—
The Unsolved Murder (1922)

William Desmond Taylor—Silver Screen Cinema Collection

The Murder

It was February 1, 1922, and an unusually cold night for Los Angeles. Despite the fact that this was during prohibition, director William Desmond Taylor and silent film comedienne Mabel Normand enjoyed Orange Blossom Gin cocktails and discussed Nietzsche, Freud, and movies. Mabel played comic riffs on the piano. At about a quarter to eight in the evening, he walked her to her car, leaving the door open or unlocked to his exclusive Alvarado Street bungalow. As her chauffeur drove off, they blew kisses at one another. With the exception of the murderer, Mabel Normand was the last person to see William Desmond Taylor alive.

Taylor went back into his apartment, and at about eight o'clock what was thought to be a car backfire was heard by the neighbors. Faith MacLean went to the window and saw what she at first believed to be a man in a long coat wearing a muffler or with his collar turned up and a plaid cap over his face in front of Taylor's bungalow. He looked at

The Bungalow on Alvarado Street—Silver Screen Cinema Collection

her and casually went back inside as if he'd forgotten something. Later she said this person had an "effeminate walk" and was "funny looking." More than a decade later, when pressed by the sheriff and asked if she could be certain it was a man that she saw, MacLean answered she could not, during her grand jury testimony. Another neighbor, Hazel Gillon, stated that she just saw a dark figure after hearing the car backfire.

All was deadly quiet on Alvarado Street until half past seven the next day, when Taylor's houseman, Henry Peavey, arrived at the bungalow and found Taylor, forty-nine, lying dead in the living room. Peavey screamed, ran out into the courtyard, and chaos ensued, as it was the studio that was called first and not the police. Originally, it was thought that Taylor might have died of natural causes, but once he was turned over, it was evident that he was lying in a pool of blood…shot once in the back.

Studio Cover-Up

Representatives from Paramount Studios, where Taylor was employed, came out and seized all the letters they could find (with the exception of some Taylor had hidden in his riding boots) and all the bootleg liquor. They even instructed Peavey to clean up the blood and the apartment.

The fledgling motion picture industry was in peril as this was during the time of the rape/murder trial of comedian Fatty Arbuckle (who was finally acquitted after three trials, yet his career was ruined). There were also the drug addictions of actors Wallace Reid and Jack Pickford (Mary's brother) and the mysterious death by poison of Pickford's wife, actress Olive Thomas. Women's clubs and religious groups were up in arms against the film industry and were threatening to boycott films. By the time the Los Angeles Police Department detectives arrived, the Taylor crime scene was severely compromised.

Who was William Desmond Taylor?

William Desmond Taylor Circa 1920—
Silver Screen Cinema Collection

William Desmond Taylor was born William Cunningham Deane-Tanner in Carlow, Ireland, on April 26, 1872. He left home at the age of eighteen after a falling-out with his father. Taylor immigrated to the United States, working as an engineer, a gold miner in Alaska, an antique dealer, and finally an actor in New York. In 1901 he married Ethel May Harrison, and in 1903 a daughter, Ethel Daisy Deane-Tanner, was born. Not able to support his family as an actor, this was the period when Taylor worked as an antique dealer in a business financed by his father-in-law. In 1908 he went to lunch and never returned, walking out of his wife's and daughter's lives without a word.

In 1912 he arrived in California and began his career as a silent film actor and later as a director. He left Hollywood briefly to serve in the British Army during World War I and returned to his career as a director. His most famous films were based on literary works, such as *Tom Sawyer* (1917), *Anne of Green Gables* (1919), and *Huckleberry Finn* (1920).

William Desmond Taylor had a younger brother, Denis Deane-Tanner, who followed in his brother's footsteps in the antique business and also is said to have come to Hollywood and worked for his brother in an unofficial capacity. Some say that Denis Deane-Tanner played the blacksmith in one of Taylor's most popular films as an actor, *Captain Alvarez* (1914).

The younger brother also followed his brother's lead in deserting his wife Ada and two daughters in 1912. After a visit from his brother's wife, Taylor paid Ada fifty dollars a month, as they were destitute. Taylor's own wife, Ethel, who eventually obtained a divorce and remarried, saw Taylor in *Captain Alvarez* at a movie theater. Ethel told her daughter Daisy that the handsome actor was her father. Daisy then began a correspondence with her father and later visited with him. Amazingly, there was no evidence of hard feelings from Taylor's ex-wife or daughter, considering the fact that he had deserted them.

Mabel Normand, the lovely, doe-eyed, brunette actress who was with Taylor on his last night alive,

Taylor as Captain Alvarez in 1914—
Silver Screen Cinema Collection

was never a serious suspect in the Taylor case, although she was very intent on getting back letters that she had written Taylor. She told officials that she had returned to the house to get the letters saying, "Not that they meant anything to anyone but us, but I feared that they might fall into other hands and be misconstrued."

Mabel Normand—
Silver Screen Cinema Collection

While Mabel Normand may not have pulled the trigger, there is a theory that Taylor's death might have been a result of his trying to help Normand kick her addictions to cocaine and opium. Taylor arranged a stay for Normand at a facility…that must have been one of the first cases of a celebrated film actor going into rehab. So intent was Taylor on keeping drug pushers away from the studios and actors, including Normand, that he headed a commission against drugs of which he was chairman of the board. Normand alone is said to have spent about $2,000.00 a month (and this was the 1920s) on drugs. Taylor definitely tampered with the drug dealers' business, which was, and still would be, a very dangerous thing to do. In Robert Giroux's book, *Deed of Death* (1990),[1] he theorizes that a professional hit man killed Taylor because of his "take charge" opposition against drug dealers.

Her body in a weakened state from past abuses of drugs and alcohol, Normand, by all accounts a warm and generous friend to many, including William Desmond Taylor, died of tuberculosis in 1930. It's been said that one of her last statements was, "I wonder who killed poor Bill Taylor?"

Mary Miles Minter—Suspect

Mary Miles Minter, the golden-haired actress with astonishingly beautiful blue eyes, adored William Desmond Taylor. Just twenty years old at the time of the murder, she had written him letters professing her

---

[1]   Giroux, Robert. *A Deed of Death*. New York: Knopf, 1st ed., 1990.

undying love. Some of these letters were made public after the murder, but they were written in a schoolgirl crush fashion and were hardly lurid. Of course, these were only the letters made public. Who knows what letters were taken from the crime scene by the studio before the police arrived? Even decades later she would refer to Taylor as "my mate" and claim they were engaged, which was not true.

Handkerchiefs embroidered with the initials MMM and a pink nightgown that was said to be hers were found at Taylor's bungalow. Actually, the nightgown did not have any identification on it. At one point, Minter issued a challenge that she would give $1,000.00 to anyone

Mary Miles Minter—
Silver Screen Cinema Collection

who could produce this nightgown with her initials. Given her strong feelings for Taylor, in a way she probably wished that it had existed.

Minter had visited Taylor on more than one occasion, slipping out of the house late at night after her mother Charlotte Shelby (who kept a very close watch on her), grandmother Julia, and sister Margaret were asleep. She threw herself at Taylor while he reportedly tried to let her down gently, explaining that he was old enough to be her father. On the day of the murder, when a friend asked Taylor how Minter was, he answered wearily, "She's all tonsillitis and temperament."

Ed C. King, a special investigator with the Los Angeles District Attorney's office, stated in an article for *True Detective Magazine* in 1930 that Taylor was troubled by Minter's unyielding infatuation. King interviewed Arthur Hoyt, Taylor's friend, with whom he worked out at the Los Angeles Athletic Club, in connection with the case. An excerpt follows:

Taylor swore Hoyt to secrecy, saying that if he would promise not to breathe it to a living soul, he would tell him something that was causing him a great deal of worry. Mr. Taylor then told Mr. Hoyt that the dearest, sweetest little girl in the world was in love with him, and that he was old enough to be her father. This little girl was madly in love with him—had been to his apartment the night before, coming at nearly three o'clock in the morning. She had insisted on remaining. He had insisted on her going home, whereupon this little girl had cried and threatened that if he tried to put her out, she would scream and cause a scene.

"This, of course, Mr. Taylor wanted to avoid, as he had many friends in the neighborhood. He finally persuaded her to leave, driving her to her home. Mr. Taylor stated to his friend Hoyt that this little girl had become so infatuated with him that it was really becoming serious. He was worried and didn't know what to do about it.

Mary Miles Minter and William Desmond Taylor in 1922 - Image by © Bettmann/CORBIS—(© Corbis)

"She stated that she had not seen Mr. Taylor for a long time, the last time being on the streets of Los Angeles. Mr. Taylor was in his own car and she in hers. They merely waved to each other. This statement was not true. We were able to prove that she had been in his apartment many times and had actually been there the night of the murder."

Three long blonde hairs were found on Taylor's jacket and were determined by the police to be those of Mary Miles Minter by matching them with hairs left in her brush at the studio. Taylor was meticulous about his clothes and had his jacket brushed every day. There are two versions of

Taylor's seeing Minter while driving the day of the murder. The first is that they passed and waved while driving, and another that they stopped their cars and greeted each other. If it was the latter scenario, then Minter could have hugged Taylor and that would explain the hairs on his jacket.

Charles Higham, in his book *Murder in Hollywood: Solving a Silent Screen Mystery* (2004), theorizes that the backfire heard by the neighbors at Alvarado Court was just that and that the person seen leaving Taylor's bungalow was a visitor that Taylor got rid of quickly, as he had planned on working on his taxes that evening[2]. Higham believes that Mary Miles Minter visited Taylor late at night. She threw herself at him once again… this time threatening to shoot him or herself. He embraced her to calm her down, and the gun accidentally went off.

The bullet hole in Taylor's jacket and vest were not aligned. The powder burns indicated that Taylor was shot at close range with his left arm raised as if in an embrace. The person who shot Taylor had to be just a little over five feet tall (which describes every female suspect in this case) or would have had to crouch on the ground and shoot Taylor at an angle.

There had been an incident in 1920 when Minter had a tantrum while locked in her room with her mother's gun, and shots were fired. Minter played "dead," and when the family came in, she jumped up and laughed. Higham believes she was using the gun to get her way with Taylor just as she tried to do with her family a couple of years before. In the rafters of the home where the Shelby family lived at the time of the "fake suicide" incident was found an unfired soft-nosed lead bullet that "was the same type and weight as the fatal bullet, which was extracted from Taylor's body," according to Detective Lt. Sanderson in the 1937 grand jury testimony.

It's said that the reason that Minter or Shelby were never prosecuted at the time of the murder was that Shelby was a close friend of District Attorney Thomas Lee Woolwine. It's alleged that Shelby may have paid off not only Woolwine (accused of bribery in 1915) but successive District Attorneys Asa Keyes (later convicted of bribery in another case) and possibly Buron Fitts (indicted in 1934 for bribery and perjury in another

---

2   Higham, Charles. *Murder in Hollywood, Solving a Silent Screen Mystery*. Madison, WI: University of Wisconsin Press, 2006.

case). In the Shelby/Minter family accounts, there was $750,000.00 never declared to the IRS. Transfers beginning in 1922 were made to negotiable bonds and stock certificates with no written trail as detailed in 1931 litigation between Shelby and her accountant Les Henry. Henry claimed the money went for police and press protection. Henry was convicted of improper financial transactions but not of stealing the money. In addition, Woolwine had benefited from contributions from the studios during his campaign (and some say after) and wished to protect the studio at all costs. According to Higham's book, Woolwine didn't believe women on a jury would ever find angel-faced Mary Miles Minter or any other woman guilty of murder, let alone sentence her to death. Woolwine was worried about his political future if he lost the conviction. More than one police detective stated that every time they got close to solving the case, they were either told to "lay off" or "you're going in the wrong direction."

The one big hole in Higham's theory is that no one heard a gunshot late in the night. The gunshot was heard shortly before eight o'clock in the evening. If Minter did commit the murder, she had to have been hiding in the Taylor bungalow the entire time of Mabel Normand's visit or slipped in while the door was unlocked or open and Taylor had walked Normand to her car.

Charlotte Shelby—Suspect

In Sidney D. Kirkpatrick's book *Cast of Killers* (1986), largely based on research and interviews conducted by director King Vidor who was fascinated with the Taylor case, it is theorized that Charlotte Shelby, mother of Mary Miles Minter, killed William Desmond Taylor[3]. The theory is that Shelby, dressed as a man, slipped into Taylor's bungalow, found Mary there, and shot Taylor.

To say that Charlotte Shelby was possessive of her daughter Mary Miles Minter would be an understatement. In the classic tale of a stage mother, Shelby had wanted to go on the stage herself but lacked the talent to be a success. Instead, she lived vicariously through her daughter who began acting as a child. At all costs, Shelby wanted to protect her investment.

---

[3]   Kirkpatrick, Sidney D. *A Cast of Killers*. NY: 186 Dutton, NY, 1st ed., 1986.

When Minter was still a teenager, she became involved with director James Kirkwood and reportedly became pregnant. Shelby paid for the abortion and is said to have threatened Kirkwood with the .38 revolver. During the making of *A Cumberland Romance* (1920), Shelby charged into Mary's dressing room with the Smith and Wesson revolver, catching actor Monte Blue and her daughter in a passionate embrace. Blue ran out of the room, and Shelby took Mary home. Reportedly, later on, Shelby is said to have burst into Taylor's office and

Charlotte Shelby—
Silver Screen Cinema Collection

screamed, "If I ever catch you hanging around Mary again, I'll blow your goddamned brains out." Just about any man who showed an interest in Mary, or that Mary herself had a crush on, was a target for Shelby's wrath.

And last but not least, in 1920, Charlotte Shelby showed up at Taylor's Bungalow late one night with her 1912 .38 Smith & Wesson blue steel revolver tucked in the long sleeve of her gown demanding to know whether Mary was there (according to testimony of Chauncey Eaton, her chauffeur). Fortunately for Taylor, at least in 1920, Minter was not there.

It wasn't until 1937 that Shelby was questioned in the Taylor case. This was a result of a civil lawsuit between Shelby and her other daughter, Margaret Filmore, who testified: "I protected her (Charlotte) against the Taylor murder case." This testimony spurred on the grand jury inquiry where Filmore stated that Shelby was not home the night of the murder and that she was afraid Mary would run off with Taylor. Strangely enough, Shelby insisted on the grand jury inquiry to clear her name after her daughter Margaret's accusation.

Shelby's non-family member alibi for the night of the murder was actor Carl Stockdale, who it has been alleged in Higham's book, accepted a lifetime income for saying that he was with Shelby between seven thirty and nine thirty in the evening. Charlotte Shelby paid Carl Stockdale $200.00 a month for life...why?

The Formidable Shelby Women—
Silver Screen Cinema Collection

Shelby's mother and Minter's grandmother, Julia Miles, is said to have taken the infamous revolver and thrown it in a bayou near her plantation in Louisiana in August, 1922. In *Cast of Killers,* an interview between Detective Lt. Sanderson and director King Vidor reveals that the gun was later retrieved from the bayou. In 1973 former District Attorney Buron Fitts killed himself with an identical .38 Smith & Wesson revolver that hasn't been seen since.

In 1926 District Attorney Asa Keyes questioned Mary Miles Minter, asking if she ever heard her mother threaten to kill William Desmond Taylor. While Minter said she did not believe her mother was the murderer, she did answer, "Not definitely. She may have said, 'I'll kill him...I'll kill him'...she was like that. She was always going to kill somebody."

Edward Sands—Suspect

William Desmond Taylor had the misfortune of hiring sociopath Edward Sands, a.k.a. Edward Snyder, as his houseman in 1920. Sands pretended to be British, a cockney; actually he was born in Ohio.

In the days before employee background checks, how was Taylor to know that Sands had deserted from the navy and re-enlisted using different names? Sands was charged with fraud and embezzlement in 1915. He was dishonorably discharged after one year of hard labor in 1916. Later he enlisted in the US Naval Reserve in 1917 and stole and wrecked an automobile. He got off, saying he'd pay for the damages and then deserted, saying they could come after him if they wanted the money. In 1919 he enlisted in the navy again and was assigned to the finance office, of all places. He forged a check payable to himself for $481.53 and then forged his own discharge papers!

The first year of Sands's employment with Taylor was relatively smooth. He, in fact, seemed to adore his employer, even offering himself as a slave for life. However, in 1921 when Taylor took a trip to Europe, Sands forged $5,000.00 in checks and stole and wrecked Taylor's car. Sands also stole jewelry and Taylor's Russian gold-tipped cigarettes. A few months later, Taylor came home and found the distinctive cigarettes smoked and crushed on the porch, indicating that Sands had come back to the bungalow. Sands had also mailed the pawn tickets for the jewelry back to Taylor under his real name, William C. Deane-Tanner, with a note: "So sorry to inconvenience you even temporarily. Also observe the lesson of the forced sale of assets. A Merry Xmas and a happy and prosperous New Year. Alias Jimmy V." Handwriting analysis confirmed the note was written by Sands. This also shows that Sands knew Taylor's true identity.

In a *Los Angeles Times* article from 1922, Taylor's friend Julia Crawford Ivers said, "There never was a more devoted man serving another than this man Sands during the first year and a half of his service for Mr. Taylor.

Mr. Taylor trusted him with everything. Sands read everything he could find. He used to study into the late hours of the night, and when Mr. Taylor told me of the various actions attributed to Sands, we all decided the man must have become deranged…"

Before the murder, Taylor had been troubled with phone calls. Someone had been calling him late at night and would hang up. It seemed as if they were checking to see if he was home. The night before Taylor's murder, he had shown his tax accountant Marjorie Berger, $5,000.00 in cash that he kept. The $5,000.00 was not found after Taylor's death. Yet on his body was $78.00 and his diamond ring. No other valuables were taken.

It would seem that Sands was the murderer, except for the fact that he signed in for work at a lumberyard in Oakland, California, on the day of the murder. The fact that Taylor didn't do more to locate him indicates that Sands may have been blackmailing him. Also, Taylor's bank accounts were surprisingly low considering his salary at the time of his death.

Margaret Gibson—
Silver Screen Cinema Collection

It has been reported that Sands was found dead from a suicide in Connecticut and that District Attorney Woolwine knew this and kept it a secret from the press to throw suspicion away from suspects in the movie industry. Woolwine continued a manhunt for a dead man.

Margaret Gibson—a.k.a. Patricia Palmer/Pat Lewis— Deathbed Confession

Having been interested in this case for decades, this author thought no new evidence would ever come to light.

14

Bruce Long, the foremost Taylor historian, who has written the book *William Desmond Taylor: A Dossier* (1991) and runs the excellent Taylorology website, received an email in 1996 from Ray Long (no relation). Ray Long had been a neighbor of a reclusive little old woman who didn't leave the house often and had her groceries delivered. This woman, whom he knew as Pat Lewis, was a widow and a friend of his mother's. One day in 1964, the poor woman, who had converted to Roman Catholicism, was having a heart attack and asked for a priest to confess to. No priest being available, she began to make her deathbed confession anyway, saying that she had once been a silent film actress and that she shot and killed a man named William Desmond Taylor. At the time, Long didn't know who William Desmond Taylor was. Long's mother revealed that one evening, she and Pat Lewis were watching *Ralph Story's Los Angeles* on television. When a piece on the Taylor murder aired, Lewis became hysterical and blurted out that she'd killed him and thought it was long forgotten. "But mother never once said a word to any of us about this incident."

Margaret Gibson, the exquisitely beautiful actress, and Pat Lewis were one and the same person. At the time she was a silent film actress, Gibson had trouble of her own, having been arrested for vagrancy connected with opium dealing in 1917. She was in what was then called a "disorderly house"…translation…a house of prostitution. At the time she said she was picking up "local color" for a movie role. Gibson was acquitted. After this incident, she changed her name to Patricia Palmer. In November 1923, she was arrested again on federal felony charges involving a blackmail and extortion ring. The district attorney dropped the charges.

Margaret Gibson did indeed work with William Desmond Taylor before World War I. In 1910 they worked together in theater in Denver and then in Hollywood films. Other than the fact that they worked together as actors years before the murder, there is no known connection between them. However, Gibson, as Patricia Palmer, was working at Paramount in 1921. Undoubtedly, she would have seen Taylor on the lot. Did Gibson have some kind of romantic obsession with Taylor as did Mary Miles Minter? Was Gibson somehow involved with a group of people in blackmailing Taylor? Given her arrests concerning blackmail and drugs, this could be a possibility. Despite women coming and going through Taylor's bungalow as if through a revolving door…there is some speculation that he might have been bisexual. It has been reported that Taylor was in an eight-year relationship with art/set director George Hopkins. If that fact had come out, Taylor's career would have been ruined.

Could the mysterious man who was seen leaving Taylor's bungalow the night of the murder have been Denis Deane-Tanner, his younger brother? The trail on Denis Deane-Tanner ends in 1930.

During his lifetime, William Desmond Taylor was described as an individual who enjoyed his solitude, good books, and most of all his work. His intelligence, sophistication, and gentlemanly manners made him a sought-after guest at gatherings where Hollywood personalities were not usually invited. Taylor was a three-term president of the Motion Picture Directors Association and tried valiantly to keep drugs out of the film industry. Unfortunately, he employed unsavory characters and became involved with emotionally unbalanced women. One of these associations, his mysterious past, or his fight against drug dealers led to his murder.

For all the notoriety of his death, the gravestone of William Desmond Taylor reads very simply:

William C. Deane-Tanner

Beloved Father of Ethel D. Deane-Tanner

Died February 1, 1922

A loving tribute from the daughter he once deserted and then reunited with.

CHAPTER 2

The Hearst Affair—the Mysterious Death of Thomas H. Ince (1924)

Just a little more than a week before Thanksgiving in 1924, while the rest of the country braved the late fall chill, Hollywood's elite were about to embark on a weekend cruise. Influential publisher William Randolph Hearst (today he would be considered a media mogul along the lines of Rupert Murdoch), and his mistress, effervescent screen comedienne Marion Davies; cinematic genius Charlie Chaplin; author Elinor Glyn; actress Margaret Livingston; and columnist Louella Parsons, among others, including Davies's sisters, boarded Hearst's 280-foot luxury yacht, the *Oneida*, that sailed from San Pedro, California.

The guest of honor for this weekend voyage was Hollywood pioneer producer-director Thomas Harper Ince, known as the "father of the Western." Ince's forty-second birthday was approximately one week before the trip, and he was to celebrate the occasion on this business/

Thomas H. Ince—
Silver Screen Cinema Collection

pleasure cruise. Ince, an independent producer, had hopes of partnering with William Randolph Hearst's Cosmopolitan Pictures.

Ince missed the yacht's sailing in San Pedro, as he was attending the premiere of his latest film, *The Mirage*. He took the train to San Diego the next day. November 16, 1924, was the kind of day Southern California is known for, just under seventy degrees, the sun glistening off the Pacific Ocean, which sparkled like limitless diamonds. A smiling Marion Davies, holding in both hands large bouquets of balloons, which whipped slightly in the sea breeze, greeted the guest of honor, Thomas Ince. This was to be a festive trip for him, a belated birthday celebration, and a possible business triumph.

Yet the next day, Ince, covered with blood, would be carried off the yacht on a stretcher accompanied by Hearst employee Dr. Daniel Carson Goodman—either the victim of a shooting or a bleeding ulcer-induced heart attack. It was announced on November 19, 1924, that Ince was dead. He was quickly cremated, and his funeral was held shortly thereafter with Marion Davies and Charlie Chaplin attending. W. R. Hearst did not attend, however; he was known to have an aversion to funerals. The rumors, which began as hushed murmurs, began to get more intense and still linger to this day. Was Thomas Ince murdered? Director D. W. Griffith, a former partner of Thomas Ince, once said, "All you have to do to make Hearst white as a ghost is mention Ince's name. There's plenty wrong there, but he's too big to touch."

The Main Players

William Randolph Hearst was sixty-one, and his mistress, Marion Davies, was twenty-seven at the time of Thomas Ince's death in 1924. Although Hearst was married with five sons, he openly lived with beautiful, blonde Davies beginning in 1919. The powerful publisher became enamored of the teenage showgirl years earlier, and their relationship endured until his death in 1951. Hearst was completely devoted to and intensely jealous of his young lover. Davies was his weakness...

Marion Davies welcoming Thomas H. Ince aboard the Oneida— Historical Editorial Archive

his vulnerability. The only time Hearst ever exhibited insecurity was with her. The one thing he could not offer was marriage, as his wife Millicent steadfastly refused to divorce him.

The year before the Ince incident, Marion Davies gave birth out of wedlock to Hearst's child, a little girl named Patricia. She was raised as the daughter of Marion's sister Rosemary Davies and her first husband George Van Cleeve. Patricia went through her life believing that Marion Davies was her aunt. CBS News reported that on her wedding day to actor Arthur Lake ("Dagwood" in the *Blondie* movie series) Hearst told her he was her father. Patricia kept the secret throughout her life. Following her death in 1993, her family announced that she was the birth daughter of William Randolph Hearst and Marion Davies.

Patricia Van Cleeve Lake, Rosemary Davies Van Cleeve, Marion Davies, and husband Horace G. Brown—Historical Editorial Archive

In Orson Welles's 1941 film *Citizen Kane*, the character of "Susan Alexander," said to be based on Davies, was portrayed as a drunken gold digger. In real life, nothing could have been further from the truth. While Davies did have a drinking problem, she was no gold digger. When Hearst suffered financial reversals (reportedly on the verge on bankruptcy) in the late 1930s, Davies liquidated stock, sold her furs and jewelry, and mortgaged real estate in order to bail Hearst out of trouble. Davies may have had a few dalliances, possibly to assuage her insecurity over the fact the he would not marry her; however, Davies truly loved Hearst and stayed with him throughout his life.

Charlie Chaplin, thirty-five years old in 1924, had already endured his share of controversy. Kenneth Anger, author of *Hollywood Babylon*, put it best: "Chaplin did not seek out scandal. Scandal came to him." In 1918 Chaplin married seventeen-year-old actress Mildred Harris because he believed her to be pregnant. She was not, and the marriage didn't last. In 1924 his sixteen-year-old girlfriend, actress Lita Grey, revealed that she was pregnant. This time it was true. It was at this same time that Chaplin was romancing Davies while Hearst was in New York. Hearst reportedly had his private detectives watching Davies and Chaplin after reading in the paper that Chaplin "was paying ardent attention" to his Marion. It is said that

Hearst, smoldering with jealousy, invited Chaplin on the weekend cruise just to be able to watch him with Davies. Days after Ince's funeral, Chaplin ran off to Mexico so he couldn't be charged with statutory rape and married pregnant Lita Grey. Grey later wrote that she was convinced that an ongoing affair was happening between Chaplin and Davies.

Thomas H. Ince was born into a stage family in Rhode Island. His parents, both actors, were British.

Gloria Swanson, Charlie Chaplin, and Marion Davies—Historical Editorial Archive

Ince began to act at the age of six and made his Broadway debut at fifteen years old. His two brothers John and Ralph were also actors. Ince began acting in movies but felt he was not leading man material and decided to turn his attention toward directing, eventually working on films in Cuba. He married Elinor "Nell" Kershaw in 1907, and they had four sons.

As a director and later producer, Ince was known as an innovator. He was the first to use what is now known as a modern "shooting script" (a screenplay with numbered scenes). He also built films around locations and hired separate writers, production managers, etc. instead of doing it all himself. In 1912 he purchased a 480-acre tract of land known as Bilson Ranch and leased land in the Pacific Highlands, up Santa Ynez Canyon between Santa Monica and Malibu. This became Inceville—his own studio. It was the first of its kind: a self-contained lot, which had everything from various architectures to offices and stage and commissaries. After his death, the studio was sold to Cecil B. DeMille, then to RKO, and was then leased to David O. Selznick. In the 1950s it became Desilu; in the 1980s Grant Tinker owned the lot; he passed it on to Sony in the early 1990s, and now it operates as the Culver Studios.

808:—Thomas Ince Studios, Washington Blvd., near Los Angeles, Calif.

Inceville—
Silver Screen Cinema Collection

Instead of using make-up to have white people portray Native Americans or Asians, Ince hired actual Sioux Indians and Asians to play the parts themselves. It would take the film industry decades to catch up with him.

In the excellent *Thomas Ince: Hollywood's Independent Pioneer,* author Brian Taves relates a funny story in which the Sioux Indians, who called Ince "The White Chief" and respected him greatly, asked for a raise from two dollars a day to three dollars a day. Ince told them he was sorry, but he couldn't give them the raise. They passed a long pipe around, and the old chief got up and began to tell Ince of the admiration they felt for him. They noticed he was the first to arrive and the last to leave and that he was kind and patient and never asked them to do anything he wouldn't do himself. The chief then said, "Mr. Ince, with this industry, this patience, this kindness, this high courage—with those qualities, if you can't make enough money out of the picture business to give us three dollars a day, then you'd better find some other business that rewards high qualities." Needless to say, they got their raise.[4]

As the Sioux Indians had noticed, Ince was an industrious hard worker and, in fact, a workaholic, a personality trait that likely led to his ulcer and heart problems at an early age.

The Official Story

In a celebratory mood at his birthday dinner aboard the *Oneida*, Ince is said to have overindulged in champagne, rich desserts, and salted almonds (all forbidden by his doctor). He then became visibly ill at the table, excused himself, and spent the night vomiting blood. It was suspected at first that he had ptomaine poisoning. Later on he admitted to Dr. Goodman, a Hearst film production manager and licensed but non-practicing physician that he had similar attacks before and complained of pains in his heart. The following morning Dr. Goodman checked on Ince and found that his condition had worsened. He loaded Ince onto a dinghy, and took him to shore and then the train station. Ince had insisted that he wanted to go home to recuperate. Not long after being loaded on the train, Ince had a heart attack and was removed from the train at Del Mar where he stayed in a hotel and told a doctor and nurse that he had drunk a considerable amount of liquor aboard the *Oneida*. His wife Nell and her eldest son William (who later became a doctor himself) took him back to his Los Angeles home in Benedict Canyon, known as "Dia Dorados," where he died within forty-eight hours. His death certificate, signed by his private physician, listed the cause of death as "due to heart disease, super induced by an attack of indigestion."

"When he arrived on board, he complained of nothing but being tired," explained Dr. Goodman. "During the day Ince discussed details of his agreement just made with International Film Corporation to produce pictures. He seemed well. He ate a hearty dinner and retired early. The next morning he and I arose early before any of the other guests to return

---

[4]   Taves, Brian. *Thomas Ince: Hollywood's Independent Pioneer.* Lexington, KY: University of Kentucky, 2011.

to Los Angeles. Ince complained that during the night he had an attack of indigestion and still felt bad. On the way to the station, he complained of a pain in the heart. We boarded the train, but at Del Mar, a heart attack came upon him. I thought it best to take him off the train and insisted upon his resting in a hotel. I telephoned Mrs. Ince that her husband was not feeling well. I called in a physician and remained myself until the afternoon, when I continued on to Los Angeles. Mr. Ince told me that he had had similar attacks before but that they had not amounted to anything. Mr. Ince gave no evidence of having had any liquor of any kind. My knowledge as a physician enabled me to diagnose acute indigestion."

Ince's body was cremated before an autopsy or official inquest could be undertaken. Nancy Ince Probert, granddaughter of Thomas and Nell Ince, has a sworn affidavit by Thomas Ince's studio manager, which states that his body was examined before it was cremated and found to be free of external injuries. On a 1998 episode of *E! Mysteries and Scandals,* Probert said, "There was absolutely nothing wrong, no injuries, no shots or bullet holes of any kind[5]."

In answer to rumors that Ince was comatose or likely already dead when removed from the *Oneida,* Probert said, "My father remembers going into his room, seeing him, talking to him…as much as you can when somebody is sick. I always remember my father telling me that he got to visit his father in the last few days."

Patricia Hearst, granddaughter of William Randolph Hearst and infamous 1970s SLA (Symbionese Liberation Army) kidnap victim who ended up joining her captors, also not surprisingly claims that her family told her the stories of the Ince murder were ridiculous and to ignore them. Yet Hearst, along with her co-author Cordelia Frances Biddle, later portrayed her grandfather as an old man jealous of his mistress and her lover Chaplin in the fictional book entitled *Murder at San Simeon.*[6]

[5]   *E! Mysteries and Scandals,* "William Randolph Hearst," "E" Entertainment Television Network, August 10, 1998

[6]   Hearst, Patricia, and Corneila Frances Bidle. *Murder at San Simeon,* New York: Pocket, 1st ed., 1997.

In Marion Davies's post-humously published autobiography *The Times We Had,* she stated that both Tom and his wife Nell were invited aboard the yacht, but Nell couldn't attend because of their son Richard's birthday. According to Davies, she asked that Ince be able to attend alone as he had been working very hard, drinking too much, and needed a rest. Davies remembered the dinner menu consisting of turkey, salad, and lobster cocktail, which did not sound too rich, and that Tom wanted to drink a toast to his young son.

Marion Davies in the 1920s—
Silver Screen Cinema Collection

Elinor Glyn said not to drink it with water because it was bad luck. Davies claimed there was no alcohol "because anywhere Mr. Hearst was, no liquor was served." Not to mention that this was during prohibition when it was illegal to drink.

It is well known that Hearst allowed one or two drinks per guest at his gatherings or dinner parties, but if guests were caught having more, they would likely not be invited again. Or if guests were at San Simeon, they would find themselves quickly escorted back to the train station. The main reason Hearst didn't tolerate excessive drinking by his guests was because he didn't want Davies to drink. Davies claimed that after Ince's death, his widow Nell said,

"If he had been drinking whiskey, that would have done it." Davies said if Ince had been drinking whiskey, he would have had to have brought it himself[7].

Davies stated that she was furious by all the rumors of Ince's death and wanted to sue the newspapers. Hearst, no stranger to publishing unsubstantiated scandals himself in his own newspapers, told Davies never to pursue litigation because it keeps the story going and makes things worse. This is an adage many actors today subscribe to.

Davies also tried to explain away the rumors by asking, "So if he had been shot, how long can one keep a bullet in his system?" Actually a bullet, depending on where it is, could be in a body for hours, days, months, and even years.

Actress Margaret Livingston, reportedly a guest on the *Oneida*, who later married bandleader Paul Whiteman, was allegedly Ince's mistress. Davies said that Nell had asked her whether Livingston was aboard, and Marion said she didn't even know her, and she was not a guest on the yacht. Charlie Chaplin would also later say that he was not aboard the *Oneida* as would Louella Parsons, who claimed she was in New York. Chaplin wrote in his autobiography that he, along with Davies and Hearst, visited Ince two weeks before he died. In actuality, Chaplin actually attended Ince's funeral just days after his death. Davies's stand-in Vera Burnett clearly recollected seeing Davies, Chaplin, and Parsons depart the studio together on their way to the yacht.

Davies also claimed that there was no weapon aboard the ship; however, Hearst was known to have a diamond-encrusted, pearl-handled revolver on the yacht. Despite his reported reverence for animals, Hearst used to shoot from the hip at innocent, serene seagulls for no apparent reason other than his own amusement and possibly that of his guests.

Chester Kempley, District Attorney for San Diego, examined the evidence at his disposal, which consisted of an interview with one person on the yacht who was willing to tell the "authorized story"—Hearst employee Dr. Goodman. None of the other guests on the *Oneida* were interviewed

---

7   Davies, Marion. *The Times We Had: Life with William Randolph Hearst*. New York: Ballantine Books, 1st ed., (March 12, 1985).

nor was any formal inquest held. District Attorney Kempley concluded the following:

"I began this investigation because of many rumors brought to my office regarding this case. I have considered the rumors until today and have decided to definitely dispose of them. There will be no further investigation of stories of drinking on board the yacht. If there are to be, then they will have to be in Los Angeles County where presumably the liquor was secured. People interested in Ince's sudden death have continued to come to me with persistent reports, and in order to satisfy them I did conduct an investigation. But after questioning the doctor and nurse who attended Mr. Ince at Del Mar, I am satisfied that his death was from ordinary causes."

In an audio interview, an older Marion Davies asked, "Who would shoot him? If anything of the sort had happened, well everybody would have been in jail wouldn't they?"[8] Perhaps…unless you had the power, money, and political influence of William Randolph Hearst.

Secondary Theories

There are a few ancillary theories on the death of Thomas Ince…most are absurd, and a couple are plausible. One ridiculous rumor, published in *Vanity Fair* in 1997, had William Randolph Hearst accidentally stabbing Thomas Ince with Marion Davies's hatpin, puncturing him in the chest and causing an instant fatal heart attack. Another theory alleged that Ince imbibed poison intended for Charlie Chaplin who was having an affair with Marion Davies at the time.

One disturbing, bizarre rumor concerned Abigail Kinsolving, Davies's secretary, who claimed she was raped by Ince and then killed him. Months later she had a baby girl. Shortly after the birth of the child, a daughter named Louise, Abigail perished in a car accident near San Simeon, leaving a suicide note with inconsistent handwriting. More than one person wrote the note. The child was later placed in an orphanage and was generously supported by Davies. These were characters Patricia Hearst later placed in a fictionalized account of the murder. While Kinsolving may have had a child out of wedlock who was supported by Davies, the criminal accusation against Ince is vicious gossip—an attempt to blend two unrelated scandals together.

---

[8]   "Captured on Film: The True Story of Marion Davies," Turner Classic Movies, 2001

Another theory is that Hearst came upon Ince and his Davies in an intimate embrace and killed him. Since Ince was trying to enter into a partnership with Hearst and allegedly had his own mistress aboard the yacht, it is highly unlikely that he would risk a business relationship by attempting to seduce Davies.

Charlie Chaplin's own biographer, Joyce Milton, claimed that Chaplin was nearly suicidal over his impending shotgun marriage to Lita Grey and could have accidentally shot Ince, with the bullet passing through a plywood partition into Ince's cabin.

Many have speculated that Hearst was not covering up a murder after all, and that he went through all the trouble to hide certain events because there was liquor on the yacht, which was illegal during prohibition. Some even thought it might have been tainted liquor that contributed to Ince's death.

The Whisper Told Most Often

William Randolph Hearst, Marion Davies,
and Charlie Chaplin in 1932 (AP Photo)

Of all the theories about Ince's death, this is the one most often repeated. Or as Peter Bogdanovich's 2001 film *The Cat's Meow,* based on the stellar play by Steven Peros begins, "History has been written in whispers. This is the whisper told most often. The yacht, you see, belonged to William Randolph Hearst."

On the special features portion of the DVD of *The Cat's Meow,* Bogdanovich related, "I thought it was an interesting story. I first heard it from Orson Welles thirty years ago. And he had heard it from Marion Davies's nephew Charlie Lederer, the screenwriter, who knew about it since he was about twelve. Not very many people know about the actual incident or ever heard of it. I certainly hadn't heard about it thirty years ago. Fate intervened, and for thirty years I had it in the back of my head simply as a good story. And then a good script arrived out of the blue."

What's interesting here is that Marion Davies denied the rumors until her dying day, yet her young nephew related the whole story, albeit not publicly.

Kirsten Dunst, who portrayed Marion Davies, and Joanna Lumley, who played Elinor Glyn, both commented on the earthquakes and storms, etc., which plagued the production in what should have been the calm, blue Mediterranean Sea of Greece: "Our shooting schedule was completely messed up because of the winds. I think Hearst was looking down and not wanting us to do certain things," said Dunst with a smile.[9]

Charlie Chaplin was known as a great ladies' man. Hearst had detectives watching Chaplin and Davies and felt his suspicions had been confirmed.

That fateful night, Hearst had noticed Davies was not in bed. He wandered about the ship searching for her. It was dark, and he saw Davies standing close to Charlie Chaplin in the galley of the yacht. Hearst grabbed his revolver and shot a man he was certain was Chaplin, only to realize it was Thomas Ince. Both were built similarly and had curly, wavy hair. Louella Parsons, at this time a fairly new writer for Hearst newspapers, witnessed the event. A cover-up ensued. Dr. Goodman checked on his patient, and very early the next morning, they moved a bloodied Ince off the ship on a stretcher, surprised to see Chaplin's Japanese servant Toraichi Kono standing next to an ambulance to take Ince to the train station. Kono saw Ince being taken off the ship bleeding profusely from a bullet hole in the head. Kono told his wife, who in turn told the other Japanese servants, a

9   *The Cat's Meow,* Lion's Gate, DVD Release September 9, 2003

few of which must have told their employers. The gossip began to spread like wildfire.

Louella Parsons, allegedly a witness to the events, is said to have shrewdly negotiated a lifetime contract with William Randolph Hearst. While she was already a writer, she became one of the two most powerful gossip columnists in Hollywood after Ince's death.

Thomas Ince's distant cousin Davette Ince has said, "I don't think Hearst had any set mission to kill Ince. I think he had more of a mission to get rid of Chaplin for having an affair with his girlfriend."[10]

An early edition of the *Los Angeles Times* (not a Hearst newspaper) boasted the headline: MOVIE PRODUCER SHOT ON HEARST YACHT. The headline disappeared from later editions following threats from Hearst. Hearst's own newspaper *The Los Angeles Examiner* ran the headline: SPECIAL CAR RUSHES STRICKEN INCE HOME FROM RANCH. For some odd reason, Hearst wanted people to think Ince was at San Simeon rather than on the *Oneida*. Ince was at San Simeon weeks before; however, too many people knew he was nowhere near San Simeon, so Hearst dropped the story.

Author and guest aboard the *Oneida*, Elinor Glyn, told actress Eleanor Boardman that everyone on the yacht, including the crew, was sworn to secrecy.[11]

"To me, it was just a story that was always going to cause a lot of debate," explained *The Cat's Meow* play author Steven Peros. "There's no smoking gun, just the smell of smoke in every room."

---

[10] *E! Mysteries and Scandals*, "William Randolph Hearst," "E" Entertainment Television Network, August 10, 1998

[11] Rosenbaum, Joseph, Hollywood Confidential
http://www.chicagoreader.com/chicago/hollywood-confidential/
Content?oid=908386

CHAPTER 3

Jean Harlow—Last Night Was Only a Comedy (1932)

Jean Harlow , Silver Screen Cinema Collection

On film she often wore white satin gowns that, combined with her ivory skin and platinum hair, gave Jean Harlow an unparalleled luminous quality. Harlow glowed from the screen, reached out and grabbed the attention of the viewer, and never lost it. She was not an unreachable goddess like Garbo but human with an earthy sense of humor, which made her a superb comedienne. As the original blonde bombshell, Harlow set the trend for actresses like Marilyn Monroe for decades to come.

Harlow remains forever young, having died at the age of twenty-six of natural causes. In addition to her untimely death, the mysterious death of her second husband, MGM producer Paul Bern, just a couple of months after her marriage, adds to her mystique. The controversy over Bern's death of a bullet in the head has not quieted over the decades. An enigmatic, supposed suicide note that people have attempted to decipher ending with the line—"you understand last night was only a comedy"—and a studio cover-up have added to the storm surrounding Bern's death. Was it suicide or murder?

Jean Harlow

Jean Harlow, an incandescent beauty, was nicknamed "the baby" by her family, and the nickname stuck with her. She was known as "the baby" around the studio. She claimed she didn't know her real name "Harlean" until she started school. Somehow the nickname suited her, and with her kewpie doll lips painted a deep red and her cherubic baby face, she played at being the femme fatale but with an underlying childlike quality and a roaring sense of humor that set her apart from her contemporaries.

No matter how tough the characters in her early films were supposed to have been, the audiences always loved her. Harlow would say about those characters, "I don't want to play hard-boiled girls. It's so different from the real me." In fact, Harlow, who was educated in upscale private schools, actually came from a fairly well-to-do family. Her grandfather did not support or approve of the idea of a movie career for his granddaughter.

Harlow was loved by the crewmembers who worked on her films. They remembered her as being very kind, down-to-earth, and a great dice player! In those pre-Las Vegas days, one of her favorite getaway spots was

Agua Caliente, a high-end Tijuana gambling resort that is still in existence. Harlow, with her heart of gold, was known to help out crewmembers who needed support financially.

Katharine Hepburn is credited with being a fashion trendsetter, wearing slacks in public at a time when most actresses would only wear skirts. Harlow also was fond of slacks. Almost all candid shots of her show her in sweaters, bell-bottoms, and tennis shoes. And her friend, Marcella Rabwin, David O. Selznick's assistant, recalled that Harlow "always had a book under her arm[12]."

In Rosalind Russell's posthumously published 1977 biography, *Life is a Banquet*, she recalled, "I was close to Jean Harlow. I loved her, and oh, she was a stunning creature! I remember sitting under a hair dryer in a beauty parlor one day and sitting next to me was a child, also under a dryer. She was wearing shorts, and her little baby legs perfectly formed, rested against the back of her chair while the nails of her little baby hands were being manicured. My word, I thought, a ten- or eleven-year-old kid having that bright red polish put on, and suddenly the hood of the dryer went up, and the child stood up, and it was Jean. She was probably twenty-three at the time, but without make-up and with no eyebrows, she looked exactly like a little kid[13]."

In addition to the classic *Dinner at Eight* (1933) with Wallace Beery and Marie Dressler, Harlow is probably best remembered for the films she made with Clark Gable, such as *Red Dust* (1933), *China Seas* (1934), and her last film *Saratoga* (1937). Gable and Harlow were a magnetic, exciting screen team. They sparked together and complimented each other in every way. Gable met his match with Harlow as his leading lady. They generated a sense of playfulness and fun in every film they made together. They represented the ideal relationship of pals as well as lovers. The two were friends off screen. Gable's wife Carole Lombard, who was unthreatened by their friendship, once commented that she loved Jean Harlow because Gable thought of her as "one of the guys."

---

[12]   *Biography*, "Jean Harlow," A & E Television Network, May 20, 1996

[13]   Russell, Rosalind. *Life is a Banquet*. New York: Random House, Inc., 1st ed., 1977.

Much has been written of Harlow's private life. Her stepfather Marino Bello was a glorified con man who embezzled from her and, among other things, invested 25 percent of her salary in non-existent Mexican gold-mines. Harlow's mother was something of an eccentric who controlled every movement her daughter made, and it is said, sabotaged her relationships with her husbands, Charles McGrew (whom Harlow married at sixteen), Paul Bern, and cameraman Hal Rosson. "Mama Jean," as she was called, would never surrender control of her daughter to anyone.

There were two men that Mama Jean found to be formidable opponents: mobster Abner "Longie" Zwillman and the love of Harlow's life, William Powell. She met Zwillman when she was just twenty years old in Chicago. Harlow's stand-in Barbara Brown remembered him as "charming" and "a regular guy." Harlow was appearing at the Oriental Theater, and her con-artist stepfather Marino Bello, in an effort to impress Al Capone and Zwillman, invited them backstage to meet her. In David Stenn's book *Bombshell: The Life of Jean Harlow*, Lina Basquette recalled, "She loved to hang out with guys from the mob. She wanted to be a rebel herself but didn't have the guts to go against her mother[14]."

Zwillman, reportedly obsessed with Harlow, helped her career by getting her a two-picture deal at Columbia by loaning studio head Harry Cohn $500,000.00. It's said that Zwillman supplemented Harlow's $250.00 a week salary and raised it to $1,000.00, paying the difference himself. He is also reported to have gifted her with a red Cadillac and jewelry.

Paul Bern

Paul Bern was born Paul Levy in 1889 in Wandsbek, northwest of Hamburg, Germany. When he was ten years old, the Levy family immigrated to New York City. As a young man, he studied at the American Academy of Dramatic Arts. He became an actor and later discovered his interest was more in screenwriting and directing. Eventually, Bern moved to Hollywood and became a producer and high-level executive at MGM, as well as a friend and advisor of "boy genius" producer Irving Thalberg.

---

[14] Stenn, David. *Bombshell: The Life of Jean Harlow*. New York: Doubleday, 1st ed., 1993.

During his time as a young actor and upcoming director in New York, Paul Bern began to date a red-haired actress named Dorothy Millette. They moved in together, and Bern listed Millette as his wife when he registered for the draft in 1917. During a federal census, they were also listed as married. Friends at the time knew Millette as Bern's wife. Family also acknowledged her as his wife; however, there is no record of their marriage. In those days, people didn't openly live together outside of wedlock. It's been speculated that because Millette was a gentile and Bern was Jewish, they never married legally. However, they lived together enough years to be considered common-law husband and wife.

The year of 1920 was a devastating year for Bern, as his mother Henrietta committed suicide, and his common-law wife Millette began exhibiting signs of depression and mental illness. She began to hear voices and felt she was in the inner circle of God. Bern's sister Friedericke described her illness as "dementia praecox," later known as schizophrenia. Bern committed Millette to the Blythewood Sanitarium in Greenwich, Connecticut, before moving to Hollywood. Millette was released from the sanitarium because she was considered "harmless," not because she was "cured." Following her stay at the sanitarium Bern paid for a hotel room for Millette at the famed Algonquin Hotel in New York. The manager there would later say that Bern visited Millette approximately twice a year.

Bern, who had a slight build, was dark and erudite. He had an intellectual demeanor and inspired trust in those who confided in him and, in fact, was known as "Hollywood's Father Confessor." He was the executive the stars went to for advice before going to Louis B. Mayer. Bern was known to lead a quiet life and at one time shared a house with actor John Gilbert and writer Carey Wilson. Gilbert at the time was dating one of the great beauties of the 1920s, actress Barbara La Marr, and after their break-up, Bern later dated La Marr himself and was also romantically linked to Joan Crawford, Mabel Normand, and fan dancer Sally Rand.

Jean Harlow and Paul Bern at Home—
Historical Editorial Archive

In 1932, forty-two-year-old Paul Bern and Jean Harlow, just twenty-one years old, worked together in *Beast of the City.* Harlow was grateful for Bern's input on her performance and felt she had improved greatly as an actress because of his advice. She began writing him letters of thanks, which touched Bern, and the two began a romantic relationship.

Harlow was offered a role in *Red-Headed Woman* and really didn't want to play a gold digger; however, she accepted the role on Bern's advice. The relationship heated up, and Bern proposed to Harlow. She didn't want to marry him until after the film was released, so people wouldn't say she was marrying Bern to further her career. They married just before the Fourth of July, 1932, and by the next holiday weekend two months later—Labor Day—Paul Bern would be dead.

The Official Story—Suicide

During the early 1930s, actors worked at least six, and sometimes seven, days a week. Harlow was working on *Red Dust* on Saturday, September 3, and was also scheduled to work Sunday.

The official story had Harlow spending Saturday night at her home where Mama Jean and Bello lived, on Club View Drive, rather than the home she shared with her husband in Benedict Canyon on Easton Drive, because she had an early call Sunday morning at the studio, and her mother's home was closer.

On Sunday night she had planned to go home to her husband; however, Mama Jean objected because Bello had planned on going fishing with Clark Gable,

Harlow's co-star in *Red Dust* before sunrise, and she wanted her daughter's company.

The butler at the Bern house, John Carmichael, reportedly heard an argument between the couple because Harlow wanted Bern to dine with her family at the house on Club View Drive, and then she was to stay and spend the night with her mother. Bern, in no mood to listen to his in-laws try to coerce his wife into deeding her home over to them and invest in Mexican goldmines, understandably refused to go.

The next morning a nude Bern allegedly put a gun to his head in front of a mirror in his wife's entirely white bedroom and shot himself. A guest book was found, and on page 13 was the following note:

Clark Gable and Jean Harlow in Red Dust (1932), Silver Screen Cinema Collection, © MGM

> *Dearest dear,*
> *Unfortunately this is the only way to make good the frightful wrong I have done you and to wipe out my abject humiliation.*
> *I love you.*
> *– Paul*
> *You understand last night was only a comedy.*

This note has been puzzling people for more than eight decades. Harlow said at the time, "I have no idea what it means. The 'frightful wrong' he (Paul) apparently thought he'd done me is a mystery." She also said that Bern had referred to his mother's suicide but never threatened to commit suicide himself. Harlow did not speak publicly of her husband's death for the remainder of her life. Her testimony regarding Bern's death was conveniently "lost."

An autopsy report noted that Bern's genitals were underdeveloped, and physicians (which MGM could well afford) said that Bern was depressed because he had "a physical condition" that made him "unfit for matrimony." At the coroner's inquest, Dr. Frank Webb, who performed the autopsy, was asked about deformities of the body. He answered, "Sexual organs showed slight underdevelopment—I would correct that. I would not say 'underdevelopment,' I would say undersized." When asked if this would indicate impotence, the doctor replied it would not.

Wedding Picture—Back Row: Irving Thalberg, Jean Bello, Marino Bello. Front Row: Jean Harlow, Norma Shearer and Paul Bern, Historical Editorial Archive

Harlow maintained that her marriage was happy, even though Mayer attempted to get her to say her marriage was not consummated. She refused Mayer's request and never betrayed her dead husband's honor.

Adding fuel to the wild speculation regarding Bern's death was a 1964 lurid fictionalized biography of Harlow. In this book, novelist Irving Shulman writes of Bern beating Harlow with a cane near her kidneys on their wedding night, which led to her own death of uremic poisoning five years later. Harlow's personal maid, Blanche Williams, was in the room next door and never heard any such thing.

Shulman also ridiculously claimed that the night before his death, Bern pranced around the bedroom wearing a huge dildo with which he tried to fulfill his marital duties. Shulman had no witnesses or sources to substantiate this, and it is pure fiction. However, for decades people have believed that this was the case. In fact, two fictionalized biographical films about Harlow (minus the fake phallus) were hurriedly released in 1965 in the wake of Shulman's book.[15]

In response to Shulman's book and films about Harlow, her good friend Myrna Loy would say, "It makes me wild when I think about the rubbish that is printed." Harlow's lover William Powell would sadly say, "She wasn't like that at all."[16]

Dorothy Millette—Suspect

When Paul Bern married Jean Harlow he had a secret…his common-law schizophrenic wife, Dorothy Millette. For years, Bern modestly supported her and visited her sparingly. She stayed in her hotel room, rarely going out, reading movie magazines and living for some sort of communication from Bern. Millette also had dreams of resuming her acting career by starring in a biblical film and joining Bern in California. Eventually, the personal contact and letters ceased. She began to get typed notes from Bern's secretary instead of private notes. It was understood that if she stayed quiet,

---

[15]   Shulman, Irving. *Harlow: An Intimate Biography*. New York: Random House, 1964

[16]   Kulzer, Dina-Marie, Portrait of Harlow: The Original Blonde Bombshell http://www.classichollywoodbios.com/jeanharlow.htm

the financial support would continue. Millette moved west and to the Plaza Hotel in San Francisco once the news of Bern's marriage to Harlow hit the press. Bern's discarded wife, tired of being exiled and angry about being replaced by a breathtaking twenty-one-year-old movie star, was beginning to circle him, and he was going to have to deal with her.

Bern knew that Millette was going to visit him on Sundaynight, September 4, and didn't expect the situation to become violent. He may have staged an argument with Harlow to have a chance to reason with Millette alone, or perhaps Harlow knew of Millette's visit and didn't want to be present.

Apparently Bern and Millette got along well until later in the night. Servants Clifton Davis and Winifred Carmichael were at Harlow's Club View Drive house earlier in the evening and returned to Bern's Easton Drive house later on. Carmichael heard a female voice she didn't recognize with Bern. First it was laughter and conversation, followed by arguing. She heard Bern scream, "Get out of my life!"

Dorothy Millette Image by © Bettmann/ CORBIS (© Corbis)

Shortly after one o'clock in the morning, Bern called the MGM Transportation Department to order a car to pick up his guest and take her to San Francisco. The limo driver later told his supervisor that his female passenger never said a word during the eight-hour drive to San Francisco, except to tell him to go faster.

A neighbor, Slavko Vorkapich, also heard an argument at the Bern house. According to Samuel Marx, MGM writer and author of *Deadly Illusions*, Vorkapich also saw a woman in all black, wearing a veil, arrive in a limousine with a driver early in the evening, and he heard a "powerful car" roar down the hill in the middle of the night. He also told Marx that Louis B. Mayer had already been there. Vorkapich had also worked at MGM. He was never questioned at the inquest.

Carmichael said she awoke to what she thought was a radio, but it was actually a scream. She went out near the pool area and saw a woman wearing a veil running down the hill dropping one of her shoes. Naturally, the servants called MGM first, rather than the police.

At the scene of the crime the next morning were found two champagne glasses (one with lipstick on it), a yellow bathing suit damp from swimming (too large to be Harlow's), and two .38 pistols. Bern's wet bathing suit was also found hanging on a hook of a closet dressing room. His body was found nude because he was drying off after his swim.

Before the police arrived, Samuel Marx was at the scene where he saw Irving Thalberg and MGM Security Officer Whitey Hendry tampering with evidence and cautioning the servants not to talk too much. Thalberg told Marx not to look at the body and suggested he go home.

Why the studio cover-up? Why make such a point of trying to make it appear as though Bern was impotent? The answer…to protect MGM. In 1960, writer Ben Hecht wrote an article stating that Bern's death was murder. His source was director Henry Hathaway who said , "Studio officials decided, sitting in a conference around his dead body, that it was better to have Paul Bern as a suicide than as a murder victim of another woman because it would be better for Jean Harlow's career that she not appear as a woman who couldn't hold a husband."[17]

This article led to the case being re-opened. However, when questioned by the district attorney, Hathaway denied knowing the facts firsthand. Hathaway later told actor Roddy McDowall, "You see, Roddy, I can't prove it, but the letters and conversations I had with Paul convinced me that this woman, Dorothy Millette, was insane. I'm sure she was the person at Paul's house the night he died."

Bern's brother Henry took issue with the claims of his brother's impotence. He said he could provide a list of women who would say otherwise.

---

[17] Fleming, E.J., *The Life and Famous Death of the MGM Director and Husband of Harlow*. Jefferson, NC: McFarland Publishers, 2009

Sally Rand admitted to a long sexual affair with Bern. And for a man who was reportedly impotent, he did seem to have women fighting over him. Actress Louise Brooks once said that Bern "got into more beds with his 'culture' than any wolf in Hollywood." It is also rumored that ZaSu Pitts's son, Donald Gallery, was actually fathered by Paul Bern.[18]

Did Dorothy Millette witness Bern commit suicide and run off screaming, or did she pull the trigger herself?

The day after Bern's death was announced, Millette checked out of her San Francisco hotel, leaving in storage luggage with a packet of letters from Bern and a yellow bathing cap that matched the bathing suit found at the scene of the crime. She bought a ticket on the riverboat the *Delta King*. A pair of shoes and a coat was found on the deck, and after at first thinking it might be prohibition frivolity, employees finally realized that a woman might have jumped overboard. When the *Delta King* arrived in Sacramento, Millette was not on board. Her body was found one week later in the Sacramento River.

A grief-stricken Jean Harlow, leaning on stepfather Marino Bello, attends husband Paul Bern's Funeral (AP Photo)

In a very sweet, touching gesture that showed what kind of person she was, Harlow paid for Millette's funeral and burial. And when she found out that there was no headstone, she paid for that as well. Harlow requested that it be pretty and that the name read "Dorothy Millette Bern." She also settled the $20,000.00 debt left by her husband.

---

[18]   E.J. Fleming, *The Life and Famous Death of the MGM Director and Husband of Harlow*. Jefferson, NC: McFarland Publishers, 2009

Three days after her husband's death, Harlow returned to work on the set of *Red Dust*. Gable said that even after collapsing on the set, Harlow continued to work and that she had "more guts than most men." Later he would say she was the bravest person he ever knew.

It has been speculated that the cryptic message (and not necessarily a suicide note) in Bern's journal might have been meant for Millette—the "frightful wrong" being his abandonment of her and his marriage to Harlow. The note was not addressed to anyone in particular but to "dearest dear."

Jean Harlow's Last Years

Following a short-lived third marriage to cameraman Hal Rosson, Harlow finally found bittersweet happiness with William Powell. She loved him, yet he would not commit to her. Harlow longed to play opposite him in the type of roles her friend Myrna Loy did. She did team with Powell in *Reckless* (1935); in that film MGM capitalized on Bern's death by having Harlow play the showgirl wife of a man who committed suicide. She also teamed with both Powell and Loy in one of the great all-time screwball comedies, *Libeled Lady* (1936).

Powell and Harlow were reportedly engaged. He gave her a 150-carat sapphire ring; however, he was not seriously interested in marrying her. The middle-aged Powell had been married and divorced from one young, blonde actress, Carole Lombard, and was hesitant about marrying another.

In her biography, *Being and Becoming*, Myrna Loy remembered a weekend trip she, Powell, and Harlow took together. Powell and Loy were films' most

William Powell and Jean Harlow,
Publicity Photo © MGM,
Silver Screen Cinema Collection

famous on-screen married couple. A San Francisco hotel manager, confusing fantasy with reality, registered "William and Myrna Powell" in one room, when it was actually Harlow and Powell who wanted to stay together. In the 1930s, with the press looking over their shoulders, they couldn't be obvious with their affair. Powell had to move to a tiny downstairs room while Loy and Harlow shared the more luxurious upstairs room.

"Bill complained bitterly, let me tell you, angling to get upstairs," remembered Loy. "The mix-up brought me one of my most cherished friendships. You would have thought Jean and I were in boarding school; we had so much fun. We'd stay up half the night talking and sipping gin, sometimes laughing, sometimes discussing more serious things. Jean was always cheerful, full of fun, but she also happened to be a sensitive woman with a great deal of self-respect. All that other stuff—that was put on. She just happened to be a good actress who created a lively characterization that exuded sex appeal."[19]

By 1937 Harlow had been complaining of health problems for some time, but apparently no one realized how serious it was. Contrary to what has been written for decades, Harlow did not suffer nephritis because of being beaten. The illness developed from a case of scarlet fever she suffered at summer camp as a teenager.

Harlow gallantly worked through illness on the film *Saratoga* until she could no longer stand the pain. She briefly visited Powell on the set of *Double Wedding* to tell him she was not feeling well and that she was going home. Despite rumors that she was denied care because of her mother's Christian Science beliefs, Mama Jean did hire nurses and grudgingly did allow doctors to examine her daughter at home. As always, she was reluctant to give up control of the situation and have Harlow hospitalized. In the days before dialysis, antibiotics, and kidney transplants, there was little anyone could have done to save her. By the time they finally got her to Good Samaritan Hospital, kidney infection had spread through her body,

[19] Loy, Myrna, and James Kotsilibas-Daviies. *Being and Becoming.* New York: Donald I. Fine, Inc., 1988.

and there Jean Harlow died at the age of twenty-six on June 7, 1937. Harlow's mother would die twenty-one years later, to the day, in the same hospital.

MGM writer Harry Ruskin recalled : "The day 'the baby' died, there wasn't one sound in the commissary for three hours…not one goddamn sound."[20]

[20]   Morella, Joe, and Edward Z. Epstein. *Gable, Lombard, Powell, and Harlow*. New York: Dell, 1975.

CHAPTER 4

Thelma Todd—The Ice Cream Blonde (1935)

Thelma Todd—Silver Screen Cinema Collection

At the lonely predawn hour of four in the morning on December 15, 1935, it was bone-chilling cold, as the waves crashed against the breakers, and the fog rolled in on Roosevelt Highway (now Pacific Coast Highway) in Santa Monica, California. A chauffeur-driven limousine made its way down the winding highway past intermittently-spaced homes festively decorated for the holidays and pulled in front of Thelma Todd's Sidewalk Café.

The breathtaking co-owner of the café, Thelma Todd, wearing $20,000.00 in jewelry, a blue sequined evening gown, mink coat and cape, and blue silk slippers, was unusually quiet during the drive home from a party in her honor given by the actor parents of seventeen-year-old Ida Lupino at the Trocadero nightclub. She asked her chauffeur to be certain to send her a bill. The chauffeur, Ernest Peters, started to walk her to the door; but she dismissed him saying, "No, never mind, not tonight," as she left the limousine and walked into the stiff, biting wind. He watched her turn the corner toward her apartment located above the café before pulling away. Peters was the last known person to see Thelma Todd alive.

The following Monday, Todd's maid Mae Whitehead drove her car up to the upper level garage and slid open the door. Her first job in the morning was to drive Todd's car down to street level so that her employer would not have to climb the 271 cement steps to her automobile. As the sun shone in the garage, Whitehead saw her employer, dressed in the same clothes as the previous Saturday night, upright yet slumped forward over the steering wheel of her chocolate-brown Lincoln Phaeton. At first she thought the twenty-nine-year-old Todd was asleep, but as she shook her to wake her up, the body felt cold, her normally ivory skin was crimson, and blood trickled from her mouth. The ignition was in the "on" position, and the car battery was dead. Whitehead ran screaming from the garage, "She's dead! She's dead! Miss Todd's dead!"

Todd, who often wore her cascading vanilla blonde curls in scoops piled high upon her head, was known as the "Ice Cream Blonde." "Hot Toddy" was another nickname she intensely disliked.

She had an infectious cheerfulness and sense of humor, which came across brilliantly on the screen. There wasn't anything unattainable or forbidding about her appearance as was the case with some glamour girls, and she had an adorable, innocent look and way about her.

Thelma Todd Dead—Crime Scene Photo

Thelma Todd was born in Lawrence, Massachusetts, in 1906 to Alice Todd and John Todd, an alderman and merchant. Her childhood was happy and her family life secure until 1925, when her younger brother William perished in a farm accident. He fell into a grain silo and was crushed to death. The boy's body was never recovered. Her broken-hearted father died just months after the tragedy.

Todd, who studied at Hood Normal College, originally planned to become a teacher. She modeled clothes to make extra money in high school and appeared in two films in Lawrence in 1923. Later she entered beauty contests, becoming "Miss Lawrence" and "Miss Massachusetts." The manager of a neighborhood theater mailed Todd's picture into Paramount Studios. The studio then sent her to the Paramount acting school in Astoria, New York. From there it was on to Hollywood where she signed a contract with Hal Roach.

From 1926 until her death, Todd appeared in more than one hundred films. The vivacious Todd had the rare combination of beauty, sex appeal, and the ability to do slapstick comedy as well as any man. Todd, with her honeyed voice and New England accent, made the transition from silent films to talkies with ease.

Groucho Marx and Thelma Todd in Monkey Business (1931), © Paramount, Silver Screen Cinema Collection

Todd teamed with comedian Charley Chase with whom she had a romantic involvement in several films. She more than held her own as a comedienne in films with Buster Keaton, Laurel and Hardy, and The Marx Brothers. Stan Laurel found her particularly endearing.

In 1932 Todd spoke to *The Charleston Gazette* of working with the Marx Brothers: "The woman who works with such comedians as the Marx Brothers must take all situations seriously. No matter what happens, her characterization does not permit her to laugh. The Marxes often insert comedy we haven't rehearsed, which is one of the reasons for their success. I've had to train myself not to see anything funny in these spontaneous bits, but I've spoiled many a scene by failing to suppress my sense of humor. The Marxes know my weakness and on the set make it a rule to do everything possible to make me laugh in the wrong places. I've almost bitten off my tongue on numerous occasions in order to keep a straight face."

The films she is most well-known for are the comedies she made with her good friend Zasu Pitts. Their teaming was patterned after Laurel and Hardy. Hal Roach used the same technique when negotiating contracts with the ladies as he did with Laurel and Hardy. Their contracts were negotiated separately. Todd's contract ended three months after Pitts's contract. Roach felt it would give the team too much power in negotiations if the contracts were to end concurrently. When Zasu Pitts left the pair's comedy short film series, New York stage actress Patsy Kelly replaced her as Todd's partner. "It was a shame to take the money,"

Kelly said , "because we laughed all the time."[21] Kelly and Todd used to watch Laurel and Hardy work, and the boys would sometimes stop by their set to give them suggestions.

Thelma Todd met director Roland West in 1930 when he cast her in the film *Corsair*. Their working relationship soon turned into a tempestuous on-and-off-again affair. Roland West was married to an actress named Jewel Carmen. He would never publicly admit to having a romantic relationship with Todd. He called her his best friend.

West was determined to make a dramatic actress out of Todd. He even had her change her name to Allison Loyd when she acted in *Corsair*. West said he changed her name so that "no taint of comedy might cling to Miss Todd's skirt."[22] Following the completion of the film, the couple went their separate ways. West went back to his wife, and Todd was romantically linked to Ronald Colman before finally rebounding into a romance with mob-connected agent Pasquale "Pat" DiCicco.

Thelma Todd and husband Pat DiCicco—
Historical Editorial Archive

21   Donati, William. *The Life and Death of Thelma Todd*. Jefferson, North Carolina: McFarland Publishers, 2012.

22   Donati, William. *The Life and Death of Thelma Todd*. Jefferson, North Carolina: McFarland Publishers, 2012.

Following a whirlwind four-month courtship, Todd married DiCicco in 1932. However, she must have had her doubts about the marriage because decades before prenuptial agreements were commonplace in the film industry, the intelligent actress, years ahead of her time, had her husband sign a pre-marital contract. Todd and DiCicco were a striking couple; however, many of Todd's friends felt he was a social climber. DiCicco's frequent absences from home and volatile temper began to destroy their relationship, and less than two years later, they would divorce.

By this time, Roland West and Todd had resumed their relationship. Todd felt that she needed another business interest and that acting was not a good long-term career for a woman because of the emphasis on age and beauty. Todd actually had what they call a "potato clause" in her contract. If she gained five or ten pounds, the studio could drop her immediately.

Lucky Luciano in 1935,
Historical Editorial Archive

Todd related the following to interviewer Nora Laing, "I realized long ago that it is only a case of a few years for an actress before she gradually loses popularity, and younger ones start to take her place. It's pretty hard to have your lifelong career at an end. They're left with nothing but a past—no future. So I decided long ago that I wasn't going to be one of them. The years are not going to bother me as they do so many of my colleagues; wrinkles won't worry me, neither will increasing weight, because as long as I can use my head, it won't matter how I look."

Her business interest was Thelma Todd's Sidewalk Café. She became partners with lover Roland West who was separated but not divorced from his wife. The three had an interesting living arrangement. West and Todd lived in separate apartments above the Café with a locked adjoining door that could slide open in order to give the appearance of propriety. West's wife Jewel Carmen lived in the family home above the café and West and Todd's apartments on Rogelo Drive.

Suspect—Lucky Luciano

One unlikely theory, explored in Andy Edmonds's 1989 book *Hot Toddy*, is that Todd's death was a mob hit. While Todd and Pat DiCicco's marriage was winding down, DiCicco introduced Todd to Charles "Lucky" Luciano, a founder of the National Crime Syndicate. According to Edmonds's information, Luciano and Todd began having an affair.

Luciano and Frank Nitti were fighting over the restaurants and nightclubs (insisting that owners buy food, liquor, etc. from mob suppliers at inflated prices), gambling operations, and unions related to motion picture theatre in Los Angeles.

Unbeknownst to Todd, Luciano's men were already forcing Roland West to buy restaurant goods from their suppliers. The next item on Luciano's list was to run a gambling establishment on the third floor of Thelma Todd's Sidewalk Café. It was considered a highly desirable location. With rich and famous movie stars already frequenting the restaurant, it would be convenient to have the casino in the same place. The film elite would likely be high rollers if gambling were available.

Not long before Todd's death, she supposedly had dinner with Luciano at the Brown Derby. Luciano pressured her about the gambling operation, "Am I going to get it or not? I'll just take it." Todd replied, "You'll open a gambling casino in my restaurant over my dead body." As she stormed out, Luciano is reported to have said, "That can be arranged."[23]

---

[23]   Edmonds, Andy. *Hot Toddy: The True Story of Hollywood's Most Sensational Murder.* New York: William Morrow & Company, 1st ed., 1989.

On December 15, after Todd returned from the Trocadero and her chauffeur left, Luciano was waiting for her. He asked her to take a drive to Santa Barbara. Deciding it would not be a good idea to refuse the crime lord, Todd got into the car with him. Witnesses claimed to have seen Todd all over town on Sunday, making phone calls and driving down the street with a dark, olive-skinned man, etc. One of the witnesses who claimed to have seen Todd driving with Luciano was Roland West's estranged wife, Jewel Carmen. She later recanted her story.

Thelma Todd, tired of being strong-armed into opening a casino, reportedly called the district attorney's office and made an appointment earlier that week. Luciano was tipped off and had a hit man beat her and place her in the car with the motor running so that Todd would never make that appointment. His concern was more than the gambling casino; Todd knew just enough about his business to cause problems and had to be eliminated.

Todd's autopsy report notes no marks of violence on her body, with the exception of the contusion on her mouth from when her head hit the steering wheel. Luciano was under police surveillance from November 1935 until his arrest in 1936. Police records indicate Luciano was in Hot Springs, Arkansas, not driving from Los Angeles to Santa Barbara with Thelma Todd.

Roland West and Café Manager R. H. W. Schafer, sitting on the running board of the car at the Todd home— Historical Editorial Archive

Accidental Death

Before Thelma Todd left for the party at the Trocadero, her lover Roland West told her to be back by two in the morning as he was going to bolt the outside door because of a rash of recent burglaries. Todd sarcastically said she'd be back at 2:05 a.m.

At the coroner's inquest, Todd's maid Mae Whitehead testified that she put one key in her employer's purse, the key to her inside apartment, because she didn't like to carry a bunch of keys around.

The following is Roland West's testimony from the coroner's inquest:

Q: Did you at any time reprimand her because she had stayed out later than certain hours that you thought were proper?

A: Not reprimand; I would talk to her. You could not reprimand Miss Todd. Miss Todd had everything a man has; she had money and plenty of everything. You could not reprimand Miss Todd; she was an individual with the strength of any man in this room.

Q: Have you ever told her if she didn't get home before two in the morning you would lock her out?

A: Yes—I didn't say I would lock her out, I said I would lock the doors; always the outside doors. And I told you, the door was locked one other Saturday night, and she wanted to get in, and she got in from some outside door.

Q: That is when she broke the windowpane?

A: That is it. She could get in better than you and I if she wanted to get in, and nobody could make her do anything she didn't want to do. You could advise her and talk to her, and she would judge what is right.

The police theory was that Todd, realizing she was locked out, had shouted, kicked, and banged on the door to no avail. She then climbed the steps to the garage and turned on the car engine to keep warm. Her blood alcohol was at .13; she became drowsy, and being intoxicated didn't realize what she was doing, and quickly died of carbon monoxide poisoning.

In a 1983 interview with William Donati, author of the oustanding *The Life and Death of Thelma Todd*, Ida Lupino said , "Certain people were incriminating a man who did not murder her at all, and she did not commit suicide…she had just gone into the garage…you get carbon monoxide and you go."[24]

Suicide was briefly considered by the police; however, everyone who knew Todd said it would be out of character…that she was happy and had no reason to end her own life.

Suspect—Roland West—Manslaughter or Murder?

Thelma Todd climbed up the 271 steps to the door and banged and kicked and screamed for Roland West to let her in. In his inquest testimony, West claimed he would not have heard her over the waves crashing on the beach. Maybe he claimed he didn't hear Thelma; however, neighbors in the area did. The door also showed recent signs of being kicked.

R. H. W. Schafer, Café Manager, Roland West, RJ Anderson, café employee and Mae Whitehead at the Inquest.—Historical Editorial Archive

---

[24] Donati, William. *The Life and Death of Thelma Todd*. Jefferson, North Carolina: McFarland Publishers, 2012

A furious Todd told West that she was going to another party later than night, and since he wouldn't let her in the apartment, she would leave immediately. West follows her and decides to teach her a lesson. He sees her in the automobile, and possibly not realizing she had started the car (or deciding to get rid of her), locks her in the garage overnight to teach her a lesson.

Todd is intoxicated, and, exhausted from climbing 271 steps, falls asleep with the engine running, and is killed from inhalation of carbon monoxide.

The next day West decides to let her out of the garage, unlocks the door, and sees that she is dead. He goes back in and does nothing, not wanting to incriminate himself and needing to think about what he should do next. The maid then discovers Todd's body Monday morning.

Reportedly, West called his good friend Joseph Schenk, head of 20th Century Fox, who helped with the cover-up. West had earlier assisted Schenk when he was in trouble with tax evasion and fraudulent stock transactions.

Schenk had friends in the sheriff's department, West confessed on December 17, and was treated with extreme leniency. The sheriff's department visited Todd's employer Hal Roach and asked, "What do you want to do?"

Roach thought about it. The movie industry did not need another scandal. West would likely get the best attorneys money could buy and probably would not be convicted, since it was manslaughter and not premeditated murder. Since no one knew about this, Roach felt that letting the matter go was in the best interest of his studio and the film industry as a whole, which had been under fire since Busby Berkley's manslaughter/drunk driving case, the unfounded accusations against Fatty Arbuckle, and the William Desmond Taylor case. West's confession was suppressed, but he was finished in the industry. He never worked in films again.

Later in life Roland West made another confession, this time on his deathbed in 1952 to actor Chester Morris, Todd's co-star in *Corsair*. Zasu Pitts's adopted son, Don Gallery, claimed Roland West also confessed the same thing to his mother.

With her business sense, beauty, and comic ability, had Thelma Todd lived, she might have had the same kind of success Lucille Ball later enjoyed. For a week following her death, all of her friends including Stan Laurel received Christmas cards and gifts. It was one last message of love from a fun-loving and generous friend. She was a great talent whose light was extinguished too soon, but as long as someone laughs at a flickering screen as she frolics with Groucho, Zasu, and Patsy, her legacy lives on.

CHAPTER 5

Joan Bennett–The Shot That Killed a Film Career (1951)

A sultry, brunette Joan Bennett, Silver Screen Cinema Collection

Studio Representative Eugene Frank, Walter Wanger, and attorney Jerry Geisler who obtained Wanger's release on bail. (AP Photo/ David F. Smith 1951)

As dusk turned to darkness on Thursday, December 13, 1951, the parking lot attendant at MCA Agency heard a loud, violent argument between two men, as well as a woman screaming, "Get away from here and leave us alone!" A gas station attendant also heard the explosive row and a woman yell "Don't! Don't!" and a man shout "Don't be silly, Walter, don't be silly." Two shots rang out. One bullet bounced off the fender of the Kelly green Cadillac convertible and grazed the man's pant leg, and the other bullet hit him in the groin, where he instantly doubled over and collapsed in agony to the ground.

Immediately, prominent producer Walter Wanger, aged fifty-six, was arrested…you see, the police department was directly across the street from the MCA building, and even *they* heard the shots. Wanger calmly told the arresting officers, "I've just shot the son-of-a-bitch who tried to break up my home."[25]

Driven by the parking lot attendant, Wanger's wife, glamorous actress Joan Bennett, forty-one, accompanied her wounded agent and lover, Jennings Lang, thirty-six, to Midway Hospital where he underwent emergency surgery.

---

[25]   Kellow, Brian. *The Bennetts: An Acting Family*. Lexington, KY: The University Press of Kentucky, 1st ed., 2004.

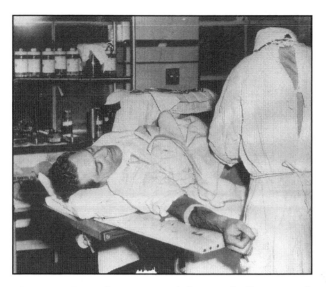

*Jennings Lang being treated for two bullet wounds
on operating table—Historical Editorial Archive*

Lang was expected at actress Jane Wyman's house for dinner where his wife Pam was waiting for him. Once notified, Pam Lang quickly arrived at the hospital escorted by Wyman, and she stayed by her errant husband's side. In fact, Pam Lang stood by her husband until her premature death in 1952 from a thyroid and heart condition.

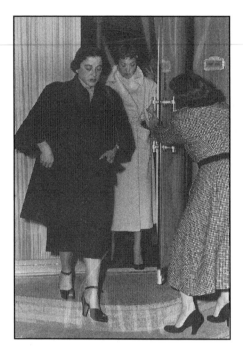

*Mrs. Pamela Lang and
Jane Wyman leave hospital.—
Historical Editorial Archive*

The lives of those in this love triangle would never be the same again. Bennett's stellar film career would virtually end; Wanger's career would enjoy a brief flourish before he was blamed for nearly bankrupting 20th Century Fox studios for the severely over-budget 1963 film *Cleopatra*, and Lang would father a child.

Joan Bennett and the Bennett Family

Joan Bennett came from a theatrical family every bit as distinguished and colorful as the Barrymores. Her father was stage matinée idol Richard Bennett, and her mother was actress and literary agent Adrienne Morrison. Joan and her older sisters, Constance and Barbara, were the fifth generation of actors on their mother's side of the family. Later Joan fondly recalled, "With all of Constance's juggling of dates over the years, I started out as the youngest, then became her twin, and finally wound up as the oldest sister."

The beautiful Bennett sisters, with their aristocratic, regal, theatrical background, were jewels of Hollywood's golden age and had that special touch of class that shines so uniquely on screen.

Their father, Richard Bennett, who came from a family of preachers, was as known for his spirited antics as his close friends Lionel and John Barrymore. Bennett was famous for having battles with critics of the day and wrote scathing letters not only when they panned his performances but when they praised them as well. The entire Bennett family was known for their arguments with the press. Once during a well-publicized dispute, Joan had a de-scented skunk delivered to powerful Hollywood columnist Hedda Hopper. Hopper later gave the skunk to James and Pamela Mason as a companion for their cats but not before christening it "Joan." Her contemporaries were shocked that Joan had the nerve to do such a thing to Hopper, who it was thought had the power to make and break careers; however, Joan had no qualms about it.

Joan's sister Constance was as assertive with studio heads as she was with the press. While negotiating a contract with Warner Brothers, being the shrewd, clever businesswoman that she was, Constance insisted that Jack

The glamorous Bennett Sisters circa 1930—
Silver Screen Cinema Collection

Warner pay her agent's fee and income tax as well as her high salary. If a male actor had managed this deal in the thirties, it would have been unusual. For a woman to orchestrate such a thing in those days was unheard of. What actor today could get the studio to pay his or her income tax off the top? When it was once commented that Constance could not take her money with her, her father Richard said, "If Constance can't take it with her, then she won't go."

Blonde, stunning, and honey-voiced Constance glided through comedies like *Merrily We Live* (1938) and *Topper* (1937) with a delightful sprite-like lightness and definite air of sophistication. Her portrayal of the merry, witty, and troublesome ghost Marion Kirby in the *Topper* films is certainly her most memorable.

Constance's stormy marriages to millionaire Peter Plant, Henri Falaise Marquis de La Coudraye, and extraordinarily handsome leading man Gilbert Roland were frequently documented in the press.

Gilbert Roland, sister-in-law Joan Bennett, and Walter Wanger enjoy an evening out.— Historical Editorial Archive

A highly skilled poker player, Constance was often permitted to play in games that were usually for men only, and more often than not, she won.

Like her father Richard and sister Joan, fiercely independent Constance loved a good fight, especially if it happened to be with critics or other members of the press. Eventually it was this defiance that alienated her from the film industry's powers-that-be and seemed also to have essentially ended her film career. One thing that can be said of her, Constance was as indifferent to their opinions on her way down as she was on her way up.

Joan Bennett, who always felt overshadowed by her sister Constance, eloquently described her in her 1970 autobiography *The Bennett Playbill*. "That beautiful sister of mine was an overwhelming and volatile mixture. One had the feeling she'd been shot from a cannon and showered her sparks over an incredulous world with no thought or care where they fell, a carbon copy of father. She was like some silvery comet who streaked through life with daring speed, the wellspring of which was an inner confidence that I deeply admired. At times, particularly in childhood, I was intimidated by her, but she dictated from an aura of affection that for me was never threatening."[26]

Joan Bennett never had any desire to become an actress; she wished only to be a wife and mother. Joan married Jack Fox at the age of sixteen, became a mother at seventeen, and was divorced by the time she was eighteen years old. In order to support herself and her first baby, Diana, Joan decided to

[26]   Bennett Joan, and Lois Kibbee. *The Bennett Playbill*. New York: Holt, Winehart & Winston, 1st ed., 1970.

try acting until something better came along.

Bennett went through two phases in her film career. During the thirties, resembling a golden-haired, porcelain Dresden doll, Joan usually played an innocent ingénue. The most memorable of these roles was her portrayal of Amy in *Little Women* (1933).

The second phase of her career began with the film *Trade Winds* (1938), where a new raven-haired Joan appeared. "After that film everyone liked me in dark hair," wrote Joan, "so I turned my hair dark and have received much better parts ever since."

Publicity Portrait of a blonde
Joan Bennett—
Silver Screen Cinema Collection

Many noticed a resemblance between Joan and Hedy Lamarr, who would later marry Joan's second husband, screenwriter Gene Markey (father of Joan's second daughter Melinda). "There must have been something to it because after *Trade Winds* was released, I was greeted as Miss Lamarr in dimly lit restaurants. Personally, I liked the idea of escaping from all that bland, blonde innocence and thought the whole thing was very funny, but I don't think Hedy found the comparisons very amusing[27]."

Because of her glamorous, new brunette look, as well as her exceptional talent, Bennett was very seriously considered for the role of Scarlett O'Hara in *Gone with the Wind* (1939). Joan claimed the part would have been hers had Vivien Leigh stayed in England.

The forties was the *film noir* decade where the alluring Bennett, with her husky voice and exotic beauty, found her niche as a femme fatale. Smart, sassy, and at times showing a touch of bitterness, Bennett was at her best in her *noir* roles directed by Viennese Fritz Lang.

---

[27]   Bennett Joan, and Lois Kibbee. *The Bennett Playbill*. New York: Holt, Winehart & Winston, 1st ed., 1970.

Joan Bennett in a publicity portrait from Man Hunt © 20ᵗʰ Century Fox— Silver Screen Cinema Collection.

The Lang films began with *Man Hunt* (1941), where Bennett gave perhaps her most poignant performance as a Cockney prostitute with a heart of gold. The next two Lang films both co-starred Edward G. Robinson and Dan Dureya: *The Woman in the Window* (1944) and *Scarlet Street* (1946), where Bennett played "Lazy Legs," a character who was obviously lackadaisical and careless to the point of sloppiness in her surroundings but managed to be unquestionably glamorous at the same time. This role was a true departure for Bennett who was a very orderly and neat individual. In *The Woman in The Window*, a painting of a gorgeous woman captivates Edward G. Robinson's character, and once he meets the model, Bennett's character, she sends him on the road to destruction.

Bennett continued with *film noir* in Jean Renoir's *Woman on the Beach* (1947) where she was a faithless wife deceiving her blind husband. She teamed with Fritz Lang once again in *Secret beyond the Door* (1948), a film somewhat reminiscent of Alfred Hitchcock's *Rebecca* where Bennett played a bride terrified of her husband. Two of her best films were Ernest Hemingway's *The Macomber Affair* (1947) where she once again portrayed a devious wife, and she gave a multi-faceted portrayal of the blackmail victim of James Mason in *The Reckless Moment* (1949).

With her third husband Wanger, Bennett had two daughters, Stephanie and Shelley. Just one year after Shelley's birth, Bennett became a grandmother at the age of thirty-nine when her eldest daughter Diana became a mother. Marlene Dietrich, consistently referred to as "The World's Most Glamorous Grandmother," sent Joan a telegram saying "Thanks for taking the heat off."

Almost directly from *film noir*, Bennett segued into playing Spencer Tracy's wife and Elizabeth Taylor's mother in the thoroughly charming comedies *Father of the Bride* (1950) and *Father's Little Dividend* (1951). The talk of making these films into a family film series along the lines of *Andy Hardy* ended with the scandal of the Jennings Lang shooting.

Walter Wanger, Joan Bennett, sister Barbara Bennett,
and Jennings Lang—Historical Editorial Archive

Walter Wanger

Walter Wanger was perhaps Hollywood's first Ivy League producer. His schooling took place in Lake Geneva, Switzerland; Heidelberg, Germany; Oxford, England; and Dartmouth.

He was among the first forty men to enlist in World War I, joining the United States aviation corps. Stationed in Italy, he became known as "the Austrian Ace" when he escaped death after crashing at least five Italian planes in practice maneuvers. Wanger then became involved with military intelligence and had hopes of a career as a diplomat.

During peacetime there wasn't much need for diplomats, so Wanger went back to his pre-war career of producing dramatic plays, eventually working in films with Paramount's Jesse Lasky in New York. Having difficulty working for the new head of Paramount and after a couple of films at MGM, Wanger became an independent producer eventually forming his own production company—Walter Wanger Productions. His first marriage to Justine Johnston ended in 1938.

Wanger's career as an independent producer was something of a roller coaster. When things were going well, his earnings were high, and when he produced a flop, it was serious to the point of insolvency.

In 1940 Joan Bennett and Walter Wanger married. He once said, "No one had ever appealed to me the way she did." According to their children, when their marriage was good; Bennett was very happy. The couple had an active social life, enjoying dinner parties and working together with their independent production company—Diana Productions, which made some of the best films of her career.

Bennett wrote of discovering evidence of Wanger's extramarital affairs just three months after they were married. She had planned on divorcing Wanger; however, a letter from her mother encouraging her daughter to stick with this third marriage and her deep attachment to Wanger convinced her to stay.

When Wanger's fortunes fell dramatically after *Joan of Arc* was released in 1948, he became deeply in debt to Bank of America. Bennett became the primary breadwinner giving her husband an allowance...and at that point, things really became untenable for the couple. As Bennett put it, "Daily, the circle of discontent widened between us."[28]

---

[28] Bennett Joan, and Lois Kibbee. *The Bennett Playbill*. New York: Holt, Winehart & Winston, 1st ed., 1970.

Jennings Lang

Originally a lawyer, Jennings Lang became a talent agent in 1938 and eventually president of the Sam Jaffe Agency before joining MCA and becoming president of MCA TV Limited.

The Langs and Wangers had been friends for several years. Lang had been trying in vain to convince the couple that television should be the next step in Bennett's career. Neither Wanger nor Bennett was too keen on the idea.

Bennett said the affair with Lang began when she was ill, and her husband was out of town. Lang made all the necessary medical arrangements for her, and at that point, their relationship turned from friendship to something more.

Bennett said that Wanger, realizing that Bennett's ardor toward him had cooled, began uttering threats to "kill anyone who threatened to break up my home," and "If you see any more of Jennings, I'll kill him."

The Shooting

On that December Thursday afternoon, Wanger drove by the MCA parking lot and saw Bennett's distinctive Kelly green Cadillac parked at the lot. He came by again a couple of hours later and saw that it was still there. Finally, by early evening, when the car was still in the parking lot, he waited for his wife and Lang to pull up in Lang's automobile.

The official version of the story is that Wanger came upon Lang standing outside of the car talking through the window to Bennett. They began to argue, and Wanger shot Lang. Bennett says she remembered that he dropped the .38 caliber automatic on the pavement and that, "I picked up the gun and threw it in the back of my car. I don't know why or even how I did it, because I've always been extremely gun shy."[29]

Bennett also recalled that her flamboyant father used to like to wave firearms about and threaten people, yet she never expected that her composed, rational husband would be the one who would actually shoot someone.

---

[29] Bennett Joan, and Lois Kibbee. *The Bennett Playbill*. New York: Holt, Winehart & Winston, 1st ed., 1970.

During questioning, Los Angeles Police Chief Anderson tried to rattle Bennett; however, she remained outwardly calm. He called her "a cool one" and after the questioning led her out through the press where she was assaulted with flash bulbs and questions from reporters. Those who telephoned the Wanger home after the shooting were told "Yes, the master is in the Lincoln Heights Jail."[30]

Whenever a Hollywood luminary was in trouble in the fifties, the cry went out to "Get Geisler!" And that's exactly what Wanger did. He hired famed attorney Jerry Geisler who handled some of the most infamous cases involving movie stars and mobsters of the fifties. Bennett chose attorney Grant Cooper as her representative. Eighteen years later, Cooper would later defend Robert Kennedy assassin Sirhan Sirhan. Jennings Lang, following successful surgery, magnanimously declined to press charges against Wanger. Everyone concerned wanted the whole incident to blow over quickly.

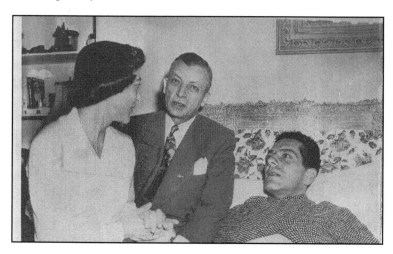

*Mrs. Pamela Lang, attorney Jake Ehrlich, and
Jennings Lang—Historical Editorial Archive*

Lang and Bennett naturally denied the affair at the time. What they didn't realize is that Wanger, a serial philanderer himself, had hired private detectives

30 Bernstein, Matthew. *Walter Wanger: Hollywood Independent*. Berkeley and Los Angeles, CA: University of California Press, 1st ed., 1994.

to follow Bennett, and he was aware of a weekly rendezvous between his wife and Lang that took place at Jay Kanter's apartment. Kanter was an MCA associate of Lang's whose apartment was used for many afternoon trysts by agency executives. This later became the premise of the Billy Wilder classic *The Apartment* (1960) with Jack Lemmon and Shirley MacLaine.

On December 18 Wanger was indicted with "assault with a deadly weapon with intent to commit murder." This could have potentially led to a fourteen-year sentence.

A group of producers, including Walt Disney, Spyros Skouras, and Samuel Goldwyn, contributed toward Wanger's defense fund. In early January 1952, Geisler entered pleas of "not guilty" and "not guilty by reasons of temporary insanity." Never mind that Wanger lay in wait for Bennett and Lang to arrive at the parking lot that evening.

According to Matthew Bernstein's book *Walter Wanger: Hollywood Independent*, Wanger asked friends Edward Lasker and Jane Greer a day after his release on bail, "Tell me the truth. Where did I hit him? No one will tell me. Did I hit what I was aiming at?"

Geisler presented his defense of Wanger with panache:

When all the facts are developed upon the trial, we are satisfied that it will be obvious to anyone that the act charged against Mr. Wanger was the climax of many unfortunate facts and circumstances over a period of time…culminating in a bluish flash through a violet haze, in the shadows of early evening in the parking lot where his wife's car was parked. The fact that the defendant fired low and that the gun contained other unused bullets, with ample opportunity on the defendant's part to fire, clearly demonstrated that the defendant was at the moment restored to full competency and normalcy…[31]

Geisler convinced Wanger to waive the trial and to take a plea of "assault with a deadly weapon." Wanger served 102 days at Wayside Honor Farm in Castaic, California. Still, with that short sentence, he tried to get out earlier on parole.

---

[31] Bernstein, Matthew. *Walter Wanger: Hollywood Independent*. Berkeley and Los Angeles, CA: University of California Press, 1st ed., 1994.

The person whose career was ruined in all this was Joan Bennett. The press read the incident as the cuckolded husband being driven mad by the adulterous wife. It wasn't taken into consideration that Wanger had cheated on Bennett since the beginning of their marriage.

As Bennett once said, "Without question the shooting scandal and resulting publicity destroyed my career in the motion picture industry. Suddenly, I was the villain of the piece, the apex of a triangle that had driven my husband to an act of violence. I might just as well have pulled the trigger myself." In those days Hollywood had a great double standard; witness the ostracization of Ingrid Bergman after giving birth to Roberto Rossellini's child out of wedlock.

Bennett made sixty-five films before the shooting and only five for the rest of her career. Among her good friends were Humphrey Bogart and Lauren Bacall. Bogart, a true friend, insisted that Bennett be cast in the major female role in *We're No Angels* (1955).

Even after serving time, Wanger would tell friends, "This wouldn't have happened in Europe. It was a crime of passion." He was even known to have a sense of humor about the situation. Once when speaking to a group of studio executives, he said, "You chaps just talk about agents; I'm the only one who ever did anything about them."[32]

Another version of the story that has persisted for years is that Lang and Bennett were in the backseat of Lang's car caught *in flagrante delicto* and that Wanger shot Lang where it counted, with Bennett saying "Oh for Christ's sake, Walter, he's ONLY an agent!"[33]

It is highly doubtful that Lang and Bennett would be engaging in heavy sexual activity in the MCA parking lot at a time when it was not completely dark and when most people are leaving to go home for the day.

In the book *It's Made to Sell—Not to Drink*, author Bill Wellman talked about driving Bennett to a lunch interview in the sixties. Wellman was making

[32] Bernstein, Matthew. *Walter Wanger: Hollywood Independent.* Berkeley and Los Angeles, CA: University of California Press, 1st ed., 1994.

[33] Avrech, Robert J., Joan Bennett Wants You to be Attractive http://www.seraphic-press.com/joan-bennett-wants-you-to-be-attractive/

small talk when Bennett said, "Mr. Wellman, I know you would like to ask me, so just blurt it out, and I'll tell you the story." So Wellman asked about the Jennings Lang shooting. And without hesitation Bennett said, "My husband caught us in the back seat in the car in the studio parking lot, and yes, he shot him directly in the crotch. The man lived, and our marriage went down the tubes."[34]

Following the shooting, Bennett allowed Wanger to live with the family, after her eight-year-old daughter asked if her father could come back home. They lived separate lives but in the same house, for the sake of the children. They finally divorced in 1965.

The shooting actually ended up helping Wanger's career. Upon his release from jail, he stated that prisons "were the nation's number one scandal. I want to do a film about it."

Upon his release from prison, Wanger produced the highly acclaimed films *Riot in Cell Block 11* (1954) and *I Want to Live* (1958) with Susan Hayward. He also had a commercial hit with *Invasion of the Body Snatchers* (1956).

Wanger found love again with blonde gossip/society columnist Aileen Mehle, known by the byline "Suzy." He passed away in 1968.

The Wanger daughters, Stephanie and Shelley, remembered that their father introduced them to a love of reading, art, and opera. Shelley Wanger told author Matthew Bernstein that her father "expanded our horizons aesthetically and intellectually."

Lang, who later produced *Airport 1975* and *Earthquake* (1974), married actress Monica Lewis in 1956. This marriage lasted until Lang's death in 1996. In Lewis's autobiography, she wrote that the rumors of Lang's injury were exaggerated. "In truth, Jennings bore a scar on his left inner thigh where the bullet actually lodged. And I can testify that nothing was lost."[35]

Lewis gave birth to a son, Anthony Rockwell "Rocky" Lang, in 1958. Today he is a director and producer and runs a publishing company.

---

[34] Wellman, W. F. Bill. *It's Made to Sell—Not to Drink*. Bloomington, IN: AuthorHouse, 1st ed., 2006.

[35] Lewis, Monica., with Dean Lamanna. *Hollywood Through My Eyes: The Life and Loves of a Golden Age Siren*, 1st ed. Brule, WI: Cable Publishing, 2011.

In the years following her separation from Wanger, Bennett had serious love affairs with actors Donald Cook and John Emery. She appeared with both on stage, and they predeceased her. In 1978 she married for the fourth and last time to movie critic David Wilde.

Bennett's daughter, Stephanie Wanger Guest, remembered that her mother had to work and take care of her two youngest daughters. There was no choice, and she had to go on following the scandal. "She went on these horrid tours, one night stands, but she did what she had to do." Bennett spent most the fifties touring in stage productions. Guest also said that the Lang shooting "destroyed a life she had carefully built up," and "that to be publicly disgraced was just devastating to her."[36]

It took until the mid-sixties before Bennett would finally break free of the scandal and get her career on track. The gothic soap opera *Dark Shadows* garnered her a whole new generation of fans. The soap's cult popularity led Bennett to once say "I positively feel like a Beatle!"

Bennett passed away in 1990 at the age of eighty.

In a 1981 interview, Bennett talked about the conservative fifties and the shooting incident. She laughed, "It would never happen that way today. If it happened today, I'd be a sensation. I'd be wanted by all studios for all pictures."[37]

Watch any one of Joan Bennett's performances, especially in *film noir*, she is absolutely still a sensation.

---

[36] Bernstein, Matthew. *Walter Wanger: Hollywood Independent.* Berkeley and Los Angeles, CA: University of California Press, 1st ed., 1994.

[37] New York Times Obituary, December 9, 1990

CHAPTER 6

Lana Turner and Johnny Stompanato—the Story You Haven't Heard (1958)

Lana Turner, Silver Screen Cinema Collection

John Garfield and Lana Turner in The Postman Always Rings Twice (1946), Silver Screen Cinema Collection © MGM

Lana Turner was the quintessential *film noir* blonde. The image that comes to mind is her 1946 performance as "Cora" in *The Postman Always Rings Twice*...as the camera slowly pans up from her open-toed high heels to her suntanned legs, white shorts, and crop top, to her white turban... she is both luminous and breathtaking. Confronted with her scheming and her whispery soft voice and supple curves, John Garfield's character is helpless against anything she might ask him to do...including killing her husband so they can start a new life.

Lana Turner's real life was no less fascinating than any of the roles she portrayed on screen. She was born Julia Jean Turner, the daughter of one-time miner and gambler, John Virgil Madison Turner, and Mildred Frances Cowan. In 1930, her father, now separated from her mother, won some money at a craps game and stuffed his winnings in his left sock. He was found dead with his left sock and shoe missing on a street corner in San Francisco. The robbery and murder of her father was never solved. Turner mentioned in her 1982 autobiography, *The Lady, The Legend, The Truth* that people had theorized that her attraction to men who were not exactly on the straight and narrow was due to the fact that her father was an occasional gambler and that he was murdered: "The connection seems obvious enough, but I can't say that it's valid."[38]

---

[38]   Turner, Lana. *The Lady, The Legend, The Truth*. New York: Dutton, 1983.

John Stompanato Jr. (called "Jack" by his family) was born in Woodstock, Illinois, the son of barber John Stompanato Sr. and Carmela, who died five days after his birth. His father and much-adored stepmother Verena raised him. She was the only mother he ever knew. Stompanato once told family friend Erlene Wille that he was uncertain whether his father was the stepfather or his mother was the stepmother. To him he just knew he was loved equally.

He graduated from Kemper Military School and then joined the marines

Johnny Stompanato, An Early Portrait—Courtesy of John and Lilly Ibrahim

where he was stationed in the South Pacific seeing action in Okinawa. He finally ended up in China in 1945 where he worked in a minor job for the government and eventually turned unsuccessfully to running nightclubs. Stompanato married a Turkish woman, Sara, before returning to Woodstock, Illinois, having a son, eventually leaving her, and then settling in Hollywood.

Sara remarried in 1954. John Stompanato III was later adopted by his stepfather Ali Ibrahim, who lovingly raised him, and he is now John Ibrahim. Sara, a delicately lovely and gentle lady, ninety-five years old at the time of our interview, remembered that Stompanato had a good heart and that he took her Muslim religion when they married. She also had some reminiscences of their wedding in China. Stompanato had apparently lied about his age to Sara, making himself older rather than younger, something he would later do with Lana Turner.

*John and Sara Stompanato/Wedding Photo
1946—Courtesy of John and Lilly Ibrahim*

Stompanato's son John Ibrahim, who bears a resemblance to his father, except with a salt and pepper beard, remembered his dad coming to see him when he was about three years old and recollected in detail a toy that he gave him. He also recalled a family story he was told about this visit. "When Mickey Cohen and my father came to Chicago, my dad came to visit us in Woodstock. The police came to the house looking for him. My grandmother had hidden my dad in the attic. The police came and asked, 'Is John Stompanato here?' Stompanato's stepmother Verena, who appeared unworried, very solicitously asked, 'No, would you like to search the house?' The police took her word for it."[39] All the while, Johnny Stompanato was in the attic.

Family friend Erlene Wille worked at the Stompanato beauty/barber shop in Woodstock and says the Stompanato family was very special in her life.

"They never had their employees call them anything except by their first names. We became like family." Wille knew Johnny Stompanato as "Jack" and his son as "Johnny."

In 1947 Jack and Sara were living in an apartment in Crystal Lake, Illinois. When Jack took off to California, I was aware of some of the problems.

Sara moved to Woodstock and lived with John Sr. and Verena and got a job. They had a good woman who took care of Johnny.

---

[39]   John Ibrahim quotes are from an interview with the author in December 2011.

When John Sr. died in 1952, Jack came home for the funeral. That is when we became more acquainted. He invited my husband and me to come visit anytime we were in California. In 1954 we took a trip to Los Angeles and looked Jack up. He was married to actress Helene Stanley at the time, and they were living with her parents. There were no cell phones or instant communication in those days, so we simply drove up to the house and went to the door unannounced. Jack was all smiles and opened his arms in welcome. We were invited in and never had such a warm feeling from the whole family.

Jack and Helene had a party for us the next night. It was a delightful evening. Jack never drank any alcoholic beverage. We talked about his son Johnny, and he said he wanted him to come visit for a month. Sara didn't think this was a good idea. Johnny was seven years old and didn't really know his father, and she felt he'd be homesick. Jack was aching to be like the father he remembered as a child.

When we returned home, Helene and I kept in touch with letters. She was a really nice person. When she wrote that she and Jack were going to get a divorce, I felt sad about that because they seemed so much in love when we were there. Helene never complained that Jack mistreated her. She did say he was not financially supportive and that he depended on her for that. She was disgusted about it. After that I did not have any personal contact with Jack.

I do know that he called his mother about having Cheryl Crane come to Woodstock to live. Verena told me that she felt she could not handle a troubled teenage girl. After the murder, she wished she had said yes that Cheryl could stay. She said that if she had, maybe Jack would still be alive.[40]

---

[40] Erlene Wille quotes from interview with author in December 2011.

Johnny Stompanato and Lana Turner at Dinner,
Historical Editorial Archive

Stompanato, known as "John Steele," "Johnny Stomp," "Johnny Valentine," and "Handsome Harry" in California, had dark, swarthy good looks and a rich, baritone voice. He was athletically built and well dressed, often wearing silk shirts and draped slacks. His good friend Mickey Cohen described him as "the most handsome man that I've ever known that was all man. No queerness about him. I didn't really believe he would fall as strongly in love with Lana Turner because I had known Johnny when he was with Ava Gardner and Janet Leigh. He took women as they came."

In fact, the very married Frank Sinatra was jealous of the attention Stompanato was paying to Ava Gardner, with whom he was having an affair at the time. Cohen recalled that while he was under twenty-four-hour surveillance, Sinatra insisted on seeing him, which was not a good idea. Sinatra said, "I want you to do me a favor. I want you to tell your guy Stompanato to stop seeing Ava Gardner." Cohen said, "This is what ya call important? I don't mix with no guys and their broads, Frank. Why don't ya go home to Nancy where you belong?" Lana Turner and Ava Gardner were great friends despite the fact that they shared many of the same men, including Artie Shaw, Frank Sinatra, Howard Hughes, and Johnny Stompanato.

Janet Leigh, in her 1984 autobiography, recalled that Johnny Stompanato pursued her in an identical way to how he would later court

Lana Turner—by sending her flowers alternating with record albums daily. Leigh wouldn't agree to date a stranger but did invite him to visit with her and her parents and then briefly dated Stompanato. When Leigh decided not to see him any longer, Stompanato said, "You won't hear from me again. I am disappointed, but I will live with your decision. Goodbye, Janet."[41] He left her like a gentleman, and Leigh never did see him again.

By the time Lana Turner and Johnny Stompanato met in the mid-1950s, both had been married several times. Stompanato, who had a thing for beautiful movie stars, pursued Lana Turner in the same way he had courted the others, with flowers and record albums. One day when she couldn't get away from the studio, he also brought Turner her favorite lunch—vermicelli in clam sauce.

Former professional fighter Jim Smith was a friend to Johnny Stompanato. Mickey Cohen also described Smith in his 1975 autobiography as "my right hand man. I couldn't get along without him."[42] In an interview with this author, Smith explained that, "Stompanato really liked Lana, but she liked Stompanato, too. He borrowed $900.00 from Mickey to buy her daughter Cheryl a horse. Lana really liked him. They were very close. Mickey made fun of him, and Johnny got kind of hurt. Mickey would say, 'Lana's too old for you…what are you doing with that broad?

Johnny Stompanato and Mickey Cohen in 1950 (AP Photo)

She's old enough to be your mother.' Johnny said, 'Come on, Mickey. I like her.' Johnny even told Smith, 'I really like that broad.' When Lana wanted Johnny to come to England, he borrowed the money from Mickey.

---

[41]   Leigh, Janet, *There Really Was a Hollywood*, New York: Doubleday, 1984.

[42]   Cohen Mickey, and John Peer Nugent. *Mickey Cohen: In My Own Words* as told to John Peer Nugent, Englewood Cliffs, New Jersey: Prentice Hall International, Inc., 1975.

"People have said he was trying to take money from Lana. He wasn't." A couple of recent books have inferred that Stompanato was a gigolo for both men and women. "He didn't do that," says Smith. "Johnny was all man. He was never around any gay men or any kind of homosexual acts. And they say he and Mickey blackmailed women. The women Johnny was with, other than Lana Turner, didn't have any money. They were waitresses…working girls. They weren't girls who had a lot of money. Who was he going to clip for money?"

Smith, with his striking good looks, suntan, and silver hair, and who is every bit as impeccably dressed as his late friend Mickey Cohen was known to be, remembered that Stompanato ran a novelty gift shop in Westwood. It has been erroneously reported for decades that Stompanato was a bodyguard to Mickey Cohen.

"Johnny didn't really work for Mickey. They were good friends. I mean, he traveled with Mickey. Sometimes Mickey took him to Chicago because Johnny's family was there. Mickey had a lot of guys who would come around, and he'd see them occasionally or once in a while. Johnny was around, and then sometimes he wasn't. He was his own man. Mickey didn't pay him anything. He didn't give him anything. He didn't work for him. But he liked him. I knew Johnny very well. He was a nice guy. He wasn't at all like they said. He was twelve or thirteen years older than me, he had a Thunderbird, and he dressed nice. He'd tell me different things," explained Smith who seemed to have admired Stompanato as an older brother figure.

"They called Johnny a bodyguard because he was a big guy, about 6'2". Mickey was small, about 5' 6". But if there was a fight, Mickey was pretty tough as far as that goes. Mickey was much tougher than Johnny was. If anything happened, Mickey would have had to protect him.

"As a matter of fact, Johnny was kind of afraid," laughed Smith. "Mickey was on the lower Sunset Strip when there were gun battles. He didn't want any part of it. Mickey's men asked why he wanted Johnny around. They were not sure, if there was a problem and somebody got killed, that he would stand up and do what he was supposed to do. It never came up.

"But one time the guys really scared him. They went up to Johnny's place and got some paint and put a black handprint on his garage. And when Johnny got home, he saw the black handprint and thought the other guys who were after Mickey were after him. And Johnny came running down and told Mickey, but Mickey knew it wasn't them and that it was a joke."[43]

Robert Taylor and Lana Turner in Johnny Eager MGM (AP 1942)

The relationship between Stompanato and Turner was intense and volatile, both physically and emotionally. While Turner was filming *Another Time, Another Place* in England in 1957, rumors got back to Stompanato that she was seeing her co-star Sean Connery. Connery told biographer Christopher Bray that he remembered going out for the evening with Turner when Stompanato showed up. "We were going to the car. And he hands me his coat. And I said, 'I don't want your coat.' 'Just look after it,' he says. I said, 'Look after your own coat for Christ's sake.'"

Connery also recalled the incident that has resulted in decades of overblown, exaggerated rumors of Stompanato pulling a gun out and threatening the actor. What actually happened, according to Connery, was: "We were halfway through the picture. He (Stompanato) was in the corridor outside Lana's dressing room. She wouldn't come out on the set...I went down to ask, 'What's the problem?' 'No discussion with you,' he said. 'Nothing to do with you.' I said, 'Surely, I am waiting on the set.'" Stompanato head butts Connery and a fight results. Connery said that eventually, "The guys in Whitehall with white raincoats (Scotland Yard) are summoned, and Stompanato is escorted from the building and deported."[44]

---

43 All Jim Smith quotes from author interview July 2011.

44 Bray, Christopher. *Sean Connery: A Biography*. New York: Pegasus, 2011.

Lana Turner, Johnny Stompanato, and fourteen-year-old Cheryl Crane at the airport in March 1958 (AP Photo)

As to the question of whether Stompanato abused Lana Turner, Jim Smith answered, "You never really know what goes on between a man and woman in their privacy. But I saw Johnny with a lot of women, and I never saw him be rough with any of them. Also, Mickey used to tell us that a real man never beats a woman. Mickey put all women up a pedestal. He wouldn't tolerate it if you even used profanity in front of a woman, let alone hit her. Johnny idolized Mickey, and I don't think he would have done that."

Although Turner and Stompanato dated openly at Hollywood hotspots such as Chasen's and the Formosa, they were not seen at industry events. The trouble between the two began when Stompanato reportedly became furious that Turner did not invite him to the Academy Awards ®. He wanted to produce movies, and he wanted to be Lana's lover out in the open for the world, not just Hollywood insiders, to see.

The official story, told for more than half a century, is that Johnny Stompanato was abusive to Lana Turner and threatened to disfigure her so she wouldn't be able to work, and also threatened her mother and daughter. Cheryl Crane, fourteen years old at the time, claimed to have overheard an argument, went downstairs to the kitchen, grabbed a knife, and stood at the door listening to Stompanato threaten Turner. As the story goes… she goes in, sees Stompanato, his arm raised as though to strike but doesn't notice his arm was raised because he was actually carrying clothes out of the room on hangers over his shoulder.

In an interview with James Ellroy for a 2011 episode of *City of Demons*, Cheryl Crane describes the incident, "Suddenly the door flies open, and I'm standing there. John is coming toward me. I think he is going to strike with his hand, and we literally walk into each other. I took a step forward, and he kept coming into me, and the knife went right into him. Everything just froze. That's when these hangers dropped, and he said 'My God, Cheryl, what have you done?'"[45]

A coroner's inquest jury found that it was justifiable homicide. "It's the first time in my life I've ever seen a dead man convicted of his own murder," Mickey Cohen said at the time. "So far as that jury's concerned, Johnny just walked too close to that knife."

Now for the story you haven't heard. Since April 4, 1958, the whispers have persisted that Lana Turner was the real killer of Johnny Stompanato. "The thought was, it wasn't the girl who did the killing, it was Lana Turner," says Norman Jacoby, *L. A. City News* former reporter. "I'm convinced that Lana Turner killed Johnny Stompanato," says journalist Peter Noyes. "I broke the story."[46]

Johnny Stompanato dead on the floor of Lana Turner's bedroom—Crime Scene Photo

---

45   James Ellroy's L. A. City of Demons, "The Scandal Rags," Investigation Discovery Channel, January 26, 2011
46   *Rogue's Gallery*, Mickey Cohen, Andrew Solt Productions, 1998

In his book *The Real L. A. Confidential,* Noyes remembered questioning everyone he could in Beverly Hills about whether they had seen Lana Turner and Johnny Stompanato together. Finally, he went into a hardware store and asked if Turner had shopped there. The manager replied, "Hell, yes. Just a week or so ago, she came in and bought the knife used to kill the gangster." For daring to ask Turner-Stompanato questions around town, the Beverly Hills Police took him to headquarters at city hall. Noyes told a Lieutenant Egger that he was looking into the story. "Not anymore," said Egger, "you don't have a Beverly Hills press pass." Never mind that Beverly Hills didn't issue press passes. Noyes was told to get out of town, which he did but not before reporting the story to *City News.*[47]

Noyes says the fact that Turner purchased the knife shortly before the murder was never introduced into evidence. However, Turner was asked about it. During the coroner's inquest, Turner was specifically asked about purchasing items for the new home she was moving into. Below is a transcript of the coroner questioning Lana Turner.

Q   You have seen the knife that was shown to Chief Anderson. You have seen this knife before; is that right, Miss Turner?

A   Yes.

Q   Could you tell this jury if the knife was purchased by you as part of the new utensils for this home?

A   No, it was not.

Q   How long had you had this particular knife?

A   I had never seen the knife before Friday night.

Q   Did you purchase the knife yourself?

A.   No, sir.

---

47   Noyes, Pete. *The Real L. A. Confidential.* Create-A-Space Publishing Platform, 2010.

Q   Could you tell the coroner's jury if there were some kitchen uten-
     sils in the home when you moved in?

A   It was a furnished house. There was—

Q   The coroner—Just answer the question, were there kitchen uten-
     sils in the house?

A   Yes, sir.

Q   Mr.Mcginley: Had you ever noticed whether or not this knife
     was in the kitchen before you saw it for the first time on Friday
     night, ever seen it, or noticed it?

A   No, I never noticed. I know there were some knives there.

Q   Do you recall using any of them?

A.   No, sir.

In Lana Turner's 1982 autobiography, she specifically remembers buying household items including a carving set at Pioneer Hardware on March
31, 1958, with Stompanato. Strange that she didn't remember that just
weeks after buying the knives but managed to remember nearly thirty years
later. Inquest testimony revealed that the nearly foot-long knife was purchased at Pioneer Hardware, as the price label was in the identical spot as
the label on other knives in the store.

The argument on Good Friday apparently ensued because Lana Turner
claimed that she did not know how old Stompanato really was (he told her
he was ten years older than he was). A guest at her home who had gone to
military school with Stompanato let out the information of his real age.
Turner was also supposedly upset that for a long time she believed he was
"John Steele" with no ties to the syndicate.

"Lana kept giving story after story about how Stompanato beat her
and was brutal to her," states Jim Smith. "She said she didn't know who he
was and didn't know he was associated with Mickey. All those stories were
lies. Lana knew everything there was to know. She knew Mickey before
she knew Stompanato. Mickey was in prison when she met Stompanato.
Mickey knew her ex-husband Steven Crane because he had the Luau

restaurant on Rodeo Drive." Mickey Cohen actually hosted a champagne wedding breakfast for Steve Crane and Lana Turner when they got married in the 1940s.

"Now Lana always said she was trying to get away from Johnny, she was scared to death of him, said he'd scar her face, he'd murder her…all of that was baloney," continued Smith. "Mickey finally got so sick of it that he went into Johnny's apartment and got the love letters she had written to Johnny." Cohen later released these to the press.

"Lana said she didn't know who he was. He did use the alias John Steele…but she knew. She even called Mickey's apartment on Barrington one day. She called about three times. I got the phone, and Mickey took it and said, 'I'm talking to Johnny, can't you wait awhile? He'll be over to see you later.' And she said, 'All right.'

"Johnny brought Lana to the Formosa many times. It was a big hang-out for the mob. She knew everyone. She liked Johnny. They were very close."

In her autobiography Lana remembered, "John kept after me. I wasn't strong enough to resist. And there was another reason I didn't get help, though for a while I couldn't even admit it to myself: his consuming passion was strangely exciting. Call it forbidden fruit or whatever, but this attraction was very deep—maybe something sick within me—and my dangerous captivation went far beyond lovemaking. In fact, the sex was nothing special."[48]

Turner's passionate, explicit love letters written while she was supposedly terrified of Stompanato while in England indicate otherwise. "I thought it was fair to show that Johnny wasn't exactly 'unwelcome company' like Lana said," Mickey Cohen told the *Herald Examiner*.

Cohen gave the letters to Agnes Underwood, who was a switchboard operator at the *Examiner* when Mickey was just a paperboy. Later she became managing editor and was very prominent and respected in high society. "Mickey was offered a lot of money for those love letters, but he gave them to Agnes," explained Smith. "They showed how Lana felt about Johnny. These weren't letters from a woman who was scared to death he was going to cut her up."

---

[48]   Turner, Lana. *The Lady, The Legend, The Truth*. New York: Dutton, 1983.

Mickey Cohen, who went to Lana's Bedford Drive house on that fateful Good Friday following the murder, told Jim Smith that when he got there, attorney Jerry Geisler was already there. "Lana Turner called Geisler first and not the police. Geisler told Mickey that he couldn't bring Johnny back anyway, and there was no need to destroy Lana. And Mickey said, 'Well, all right,' because Mickey had been around a lot of death. Mickey felt bad. He liked Johnny, but he liked Geisler too. So he'd didn't want to hurt Geisler because he helped him many times in the past. But then Lana came up with these stories because she was afraid and because everybody pretty much guessed that she did it and not the kid. Geisler told them just let the kid take the rap. It won't mean anything; nothing's going to happen.

"If anything," continued Smith, "I think she was jealous, and somehow they got into an argument. Mickey thought Johnny must have been asleep; I don't know. Lana was small, frail, and thin. Even the kid…the story was that she was listening at the bedroom door and she had a knife and she ran in and stabbed him. If he sees her coming, he doesn't have to be a tough guy to throw his hands up and defend himself. It wouldn't be such a clean cut. It was a clean cut that punctured his aorta. There was no blood or anything. I have never seen anything so misinterpreted…not misinterpreted but the wrong story. But even after Mickey had Agnes Underwood print the letters, nothing still happened. We didn't know why…they just believed everything Lana said. Because of Mickey, they portrayed Johnny so badly."

A few days after the murder, Bette Davis and her husband, actor Gary Merrill, were looking for a house to rent. In his 1988 autobiography, Merrill recalled "I had the eerie feeling that I had seen this place somewhere before." He and Davis remembered that they had seen pictures of some of the rooms in the newspapers, finally realizing it was Lana Turner's home where Johnny Stompanato was murdered. "The real estate agency had been so anxious to rent it that the bloodied mattress hadn't been removed before people began to troop through." After seeing the gruesome blood-soaked mattress, Merrill said to his wife, "Let's get the hell out of here."[49]

Many, including Carmine Stompanato (Johnny's brother) and Mickey Cohen, believed that Stompanato was lying down or asleep when stabbed.

---

[49] Merrill, Gary. *Bette, Rita, and the Rest of My Life*. New York: Berkley, 1990.

John Ibrahim remembers a marine friend of his father's who told him he believed Stompanato died sleeping. "Even if you weren't in the marines, you'd get out of someone's way that had a knife," says Ibrahim. "It's so obvious to me that he was murdered and that he did not walk into the knife. Why were all these people called before the police? Lana's mother, attorney, and ex-husband…everyone was called before the police. Maybe if they had come in ten minutes, my father would still be alive. And the knife…it was all cleaned up with no fingerprints. If Cheryl had done it, there would have been fingerprints on it."

Harold Kade, MD, the medical examiner who performed Stompanato's autopsy, testified at the coroner's inquest, "The knife was not straight up, and it was angled slightly about two inches to the right of the midline. It didn't go straight in from the front to back, but it went straight into the body. It headed straight inward to the backbone."

Cheryl Crane, grandmother Mildred Turner,
and Lana Turner circa 1968—
Historical Editorial Archive

A damage suit in the amount of $750,000.00 against Lana Turner, Cheryl Crane, and Steven Crane was filed on behalf of John Ibrahim in 1958. The attorney for the Stompanato family, William Jerome Pollack, submitted a prone knifing theory. Was John Stompanato stabbed while standing up or lying down? Pollack attempted to show in a demonstration on a dummy that Stompanato must have been lying down...not standing up...when stabbed. He claimed Stompanato's fatal wound was too high up to permit Cheryl to stab him without having her hand at a "clumsy, awkward angle." The suit was eventually settled for $20,000.00 in 1961.

Eric Root, a friend and companion of Lana Turner's for more than twenty years, claimed in his 1996 book *The Private Diary of My Life with Lana* that one night while in Turner's suite at the Plaza Hotel, they were watching a documentary on Hollywood scandals that unsurprisingly featured the Stompanato murder. Root asked her if she wanted him to turn it off. She didn't answer and finally blurted out "I killed the son-of-a-bitch and I'd do it again!" Root was shocked, and then Turner dismissed what she had said.

A couple of hours later, she told Root that she was feeling guilt over her daughter and the Stompanato murder. Turner said she felt she owed Cheryl a great deal.

"I've done so many things wrong in my life I've had to live with, but darling, if I die before my daughter, you should tell the truth so I can rest in peace," said Turner. "Don't let my baby take the rap all her life for my mistake. I'll tell you something else, Eric. I do trust you. Now you know. I've spoken to you and said things I've never told anyone else, until tonight. Remember you're the only one who can set the record straight. Tell it. Someday when I'm gone—tell it all."[50]

Later, Turner let certain facts slip, such as that her young daughter did not go downstairs and get the knife from the kitchen. "I kept that knife in the nightstand. The one by my bed." On several later occasions, she told Root that she stabbed Stompanato in the bed.

---

[50] Root, Eric, Dale Crawford, and Raymond Strait. *My Private Diary of My Life with Lana*, Beverly Hills, CA: Dove Books, 1996.

Root also obtained information from Fred Otash, a private eye who was once a member of the LAPD gangster squad, through author Raymond Strait, Otash's friend and biographer from the unpublished manuscript *The Whole Truth*.

Lana Turner's attorney, Jerry Geisler, called Otash to Lana Turner's house telling him to "Get the hell over here. We've got a bloody mess on our hands. Stompanato's dead. There's blood all over the place—the bed looks like somebody butchered a hog in it." Allegedly, Geisler had already begun to tamper with the crime scene, cleaning it up, and it was a full two hours before the police were called.

According to the coroner's inquest, the fingerprints were smudged on the knife and could not be identified. There was no blood around the body, and it was a clean wound. It didn't appear that Stompanato had tried to defend himself. There wasn't any disarray in the movie star's pink bedroom. Not even a perfume bottle was turned over. Also, there were unidentified dark and light fibers and hairs embedded on the blade of the knife. During these pre-DNA testing times, nothing further was done to investigate this.

According to author Raymond Strait, Otash said, "I changed the prints myself." Someone tipped off Clinton Anderson, Beverly Hills Chief of Police, that Otash claimed to have damaging political information on Anderson. "That's the only reason he never booked me. Geisler could have lost his license and so could I—and we'd both be doing a long stretch up the road if it could be proved. Neither of us talked."[51]

Otash claimed that Lana Turner found Johnny Stompanato with Cheryl and went berserk. Crane states that she was raped by her stepfather Lex Barker but has never made any such claim about Johnny Stompanato. In fact, she says he went out of his way to avoid touching or being overly friendly with her.

When Geisler was in the hospital just prior to his death, he asked to see Otash. Geisler told Otash, "Don't ever talk about this as long as I'm alive." "Nor as long as I'm alive," Otash laughed.

For all the folklore about Johnny Stompanato, here are the facts. He was never arrested for anything that resulted in an actual conviction. He

---

[51]   Otash, Fred, and Raymond Strait. "The Whole Truth" (Unpublished).

was held for vagrancy, associating with known criminals, and traffic violations, and his record ended in 1952 for "suspicion" of robbery. FBI files indicate that he was suspected of involvement in blackmail and being a procurer/pimp, yet the US attorney declined prosecution indicating that there must not have been enough evidence to charge him. While certainly no choirboy, Stompanato was never found guilty of any of these crimes in a court of law; however, he has been maligned more years than he was alive.

"They found it justifiable homicide, and they buried his reputation," says Jim Smith. "It made Johnny out to be the worst guy that ever lived, and he wasn't that at all. He got a bad reputation by being around with Mickey, but he didn't care because he didn't really do anything. Johnny didn't deserve all that they said about him."

Crane stated in her autobiography that she felt that her lover Jocelyn "Josh" couldn't possibly care for a person who had killed someone. She made a mock confession of actually not committing murder. Crane said she had never spoken of Stompanato to Josh.

"'You know,' I began, 'I didn't do it.' She didn't react. I would have to try again. 'I love you so much more than anyone before in my life, Josh, that I don't want you to think that I could do a terrible thing like that.'"[52] Her lover replied that she thought it was very noble of Crane to come to her mother's defense.

John Ibrahim was shielded from his father's murder as a child. "I never got a chance to go to his funeral. I was eleven years old and didn't know that much about him. Then later it started coming out more. I didn't start mentioning who my father was until I was in high school. When I moved out of the house, my mom gave me this green box that said 'Stompanato' on it. It had all the magazines and his death certificate."

Whether you think Cheryl Crane committed murder in defense of Lana Turner, or you believe that she took responsibility for a murder she did not commit in order to protect her mother, she has had to endure scrutiny over this event her entire life. Lana Turner left her estate in excess of

---

52   Crane, Cheryl. *Detour: A Hollywood Story*. New York: Arbor House-Morrow, 1988.

$1 million to her maid/companion Carmen Lopez Cruz, bequeathing just $50,000.00 to her only daughter.

A boy with a green box of mementoes that included magazines filled with falsehoods smearing his father's character and a girl who either defended her mother by committing the ultimate crime or took the blame for her mother's act of rage, only to be passed over in her mother's will— they are the ones who have suffered most of all.

CHAPTER 7

George Reeves–
Who Killed Superman? (1959)

George Reeves, Silver Screen Cinema Collection

It was a perfect, cool California summer evening in 1959, when sometime after midnight a gunshot to the head ended the life of George Reeves in a small upstairs bedroom of his home, as people he hardly knew drank his liquor and partied downstairs.

The Reeves home on Benedict Canyon Drive, in the rustic terrain just above Beverly Hills, is located in a hauntingly beautiful area where in the 1930s Jean Harlow's husband Paul Bern died, and a decade after Reeves's demise, the violent Manson family massacre of gorgeous, pregnant actress Sharon Tate and her guests would shock the country. It is a private community where actors, cloistered in the hillside canyon, strangely have a sense of safety and more importantly, feel they have greater privacy than in the very public city below.

The death of George Reeves on June 16, 1959, stunned a very significant segment of the public—children. Reeves, with his muscular build, chiseled physique, lantern jaw, and warm, kind smile was best known for his portrayal of Superman on television. He was the beloved hero and even a surrogate father figure to countless children. He was supposed to be indestructible...faster than a speeding bullet. Many baby boomers can remember exactly where they were and what they were doing when they heard that Superman was dead and worse yet, supposedly at his own hand. It was, and remains, incomprehensible to them.

As much as the children loved him, Reeves cared for them. Ninety-one percent of households with children were tuned into *Superman* every week. He wouldn't don the Superman suit for public appearances but would wear the costume he despised when he visited hospitals and children's charity groups.

Apparently, the few times he did wear the costume at public appearances, a child here and there would throw rocks at him or kick him in the shins to test how indestructible Superman really was. Rumor also has it that one little boy pulled a real pistol on him because he wanted to see if bullets would really bounce off Superman. Reeves reportedly gently explained to the child that the bullets that bounced off him might hurt someone else, and the boy turned the gun over to him.

*George Reeves as Superman and Noel Neill as Lois Lane—
Silver Screen Cinema Collection*

The first time he visited an orphanage as Superman and saw the children's ecstatic reaction, Reeves was overwhelmed with emotion. Every year when shooting of the series stopped, Reeves would cut the *S* insignia out of his costume and send it to a needy or sick child as a souvenir. He would then burn the rest of his costume in frustration over being typecast. Between takes he would sit in front of an ice bucket with a fan blowing on him. The suit was made out of wool with rubber latex muscles that gave him a rash. It's said that he lost pounds of water through sweat under the lights.

George Reeves was born George Keefer Brewer to Helen Lescher and Don Brewer in Woolstock, Iowa, in 1914. The couple soon separated. In 1927 George was adopted by his stepfather, Frank Bessolo, and took his last name, becoming George Bessolo before taking the stage name Reeves.

Reeves's mother told him that his father had committed suicide by shooting himself in the head. Many years later Don Brewer tracked down Reeves, who was furious about the lie his mother had told him about his father, and he didn't speak to her for years. Their relationship would never be the same.

While at Pasadena City College, Reeves entered the Golden Gloves boxing competition. Sportswriter Mannie Pineta said that Reeves "wasn't a cream puff, but he didn't have the killer instinct you need to be a great fighter." It seems Reeves's mother was so horrified that her son was boxing that she hired a retired fighter to beat him up. Mother wanted him to know what fighting was really like. He gave up and turned his attention toward acting.

Reeves's relationship with his mother seems to have had an influence on his later relationships with women. With the exception of the only woman he ever married, Ellanora Needles (1940–1949), who was an introspective, gentle lady, Reeves had an attraction to strong, take-charge, overbearing women.

Reeves began acting at the Pasadena Community Playhouse in the 1930s. His first big screen role was as one of the red-haired Tarleton twins in *Gone With The Wind*. Fred Crane, the actor who played the other twin, remembered, "We were enough alike in size, when we dyed our hair we could pass for brothers. My first impression of the man was that he was a great person. I embraced him as a friend right away. We had fun."[53]

Reeves gave a compelling performance in *The Last Will and Testament of Tom Smith* (1943), a World War II propaganda short. Perhaps his best role was with Claudette Colbert in *So Proudly We Hail* (1943),. His portrayal of the soldier and love interest to Colbert showcased the best of his dramatic and comedic abilities.

Following this film, Reeves was drafted and joined the Air Force Special Forces. The director of *So Proudly We Hail,* Mark Sandrich, promised him stardom after the war. By the time Reeves came back from the service, Sandrich was dead. Reeves later told *Superman* co-star Jack Larson, "If Mark Sandrich hadn't died young, I wouldn't be sitting here in this monkey suit today."

---

[53] *Biography,* "George Reeves: The Perils of a Superhero", February 9, 2000

Did the man of steel, reportedly despondent over being typecast, really kill himself? The late private detective Milo Speriglio, who worked on the case for decades and was originally hired by Reeves's mother Helen Bessolo, declared, "We've come to the conclusion that George Reeves did not commit suicide. In fact, he was murdered."

Suicide or Accidental Death?

The coroner's report listed Reeves's death as "probable suicide," and the death certificate listed it as "suicide." The official story is that George Reeves was asleep. His fian-

George Reeves and Claudette Colbert in So Proudly We Hail (1943) © Paramount, Silver Screen Cinema Collection

cée, Leonore Lemmon, and Robert Condon, who was Reeves's guest and was writing his life story, were drinking in the living room. Reeves was scheduled to box a two-round exhibition with Archie Moore in San Diego and was trying to get some sleep.

The Los Angeles Police Department report states that Reeves's neighbors, Carol Von Ronkel and William Bliss, came to the house at 12:05 a.m., and Lemmon let them in. This woke Reeves up, and he became irate and told them to leave. He had words with Bliss. Both men apologized to each other and had a drink together. Suddenly, Reeves went back upstairs to go to bed. Lemmon predicted, "George is going to get a gun out of the drawer. Hear him? That George, he's going to shoot himself." Moments later they heard a shot, and Lemmon asked Bliss to go upstairs and see what happened.

Bliss entered the upstairs bedroom and observed Reeves lying nude on his back, across the bed. There was a large amount of blood on his body and head.

When the LAPD arrived, they found a .30 caliber German Luger lying on the floor between Reeves's feet. The bullet had passed through his head and lodged in the ceiling of the room. The shell casing was found under Reeves's body. The bathrobe was lying at the foot of the bed. No notes or messages were found. According to the police report, "Witnesses present stated that the decedent was quite despondent about not being able to get the type of acting work that he wanted."

In 1992 Art Weissman, Reeves's personal manager and executor of his estate, related the following to interviewer Geraldo Rivera: "I was told it was death by suicide by self-inflicted gunshot wound. I said I didn't believe it. I went to the mortuary the next morning and saw the wound and saw my friend.

George Reeves on the set of Superman with an unidentified actor, Silver Screen Cinema Collection

"George was not a believer in live ammunition in those guns because there had been a lot of parties there in the house, and he didn't like the idea of anybody picking up a gun and saying 'bang,' and so the fact that there was live ammunition in one of the guns is a problem for me to accept."[54]

Weissman also believed that Reeves's death could have been made to look like an accident by loading the gun with bullets without his knowledge. Reeves had been known to play Russian roulette with blanks.

Jack Larson, who portrayed "Jimmy Olson" on the *Superman*

---

[54] *Now it Can Be Told*, Geraldo Rivera (Host), "George Reeves," Cable News Network, 1992

series, is one of the few people who believed the suicide theory and that being typecast as Superman drove Reeves to despair as he himself was upset at being typed as "Jimmy Olsen." "I've always thought that it was suicide. I've since come to understand that possibly it wasn't. I realized there were two other bullet holes. I saw them with my own eyes. And that was the only thing for me. I can't explain that. I don't know what happened that night. No one will ever know."

The other person who believed the suicide theory was Reeves's fiancée Leonore Lemmon: "What made him commit suicide was Superman. It was as simple as that."

The LAPD closed the case within twenty-four hours. None of the witnesses were asked to testify at an inquest. Their statements at the crime scene were considered sufficient. Once Reeves's mother Helen Bessolo hired attorney Jerry Geisler, the police suddenly decided an autopsy would be a good idea. The autopsy was performed on an embalmed body, which could have compromised the findings. The extra bullet holes were never noted in the police report.

Also, Geisler, who never backed away from any case, suddenly stopped returning Bessolo's calls. He finally told her that he felt it was in everyone's best interest to end the investigation.

Author Chuck Harter related to interviewer John Craig the following facts that do not support suicide:

There were no powder burns on Reeves's hands or on his head wound, which means the gun was held at least sixteen inches away. It's very difficult to shoot yourself in this position.

The embalming took place before the autopsy, which was done late. The Luger had been recently oiled, so the police were unable to take any fingerprints. The murder weapon was found, and there were three chambers empty in the Luger. Reeves's body was found lying on top of a spent shell. The other two shells were not there. More than likely they were picked up after the murder.

Also if he were holding a gun up to his head, the shell would project forward. When they found his body, he was lying on the shell, which was on the bed behind him. The extra bullet holes were never explained. Everyone in the house was extremely drunk and disorderly. Reeves's blood alcohol level was .27 percent—three times the legal limit.

The police were not called for forty-five minutes. They were removing evidence, getting their stories straight, and sobering up enough to talk.[55]

In addition, there were bruises on Reeves's head and chest. Autopsy photos that disappeared until recently show these contusions. It's likely he didn't get these abrasions from falling on the bed. Did he engage in a struggle or was he hit on the head?

Detective Speriglio said, "We recreated the scene, and based upon the evidence, if George were to have shot himself, he would have had to have been standing on his head with his arm approximately one and half feet from his head. There were absolutely no powder burns on his face or hands, which means it was impossible for him to have shot himself.

"In the last three weeks of his life," Speriglio continued, "he went out and bought three guns, including the one that killed him. He also carried a baseball bat with him in his car."[56]

In 1995 Reeves's former wife, Ellanora Reeves Rose, told KCBS TV reporter Brad Goode, "I was a friend until his tragic death. People who never really knew him can speculate on his demise, but I am absolutely convinced that George Reeves was murdered."

The new acquaintances in his house and fiancée Lemmon claimed Reeves was depressed. Reeves's friends and co-workers say he was in good spirits. He had a tour of Australia set for August and would have earned $20,000.00.

The day before he died, he was told that *Superman* would resume. While he hated being typecast, he was excited about getting back to work and directing episodes. Reeves was set to start his own production company. He was also being considered to play Dick Tracy.

---

[55]   *Talk of The Town*, John Craig, Long Beach, California, Public Access, 1992
[56]   *Inside Edition*, "George Reeves Segment," Syndicated, 1995

Suspects—Eddie and Toni Mannix

Toni Lanier Mannix was a former Ziegfeld Girl and wife of powerful MGM executive Eddie "The Bulldog" Mannix. The allegedly mob-connected Mannix, along with MGM publicity chief Howard Strickling, were known as "fixers." If a star got in trouble, they "fixed" and/or covered up the situation and kept it out of the press.

Toni Mannix and George Reeves began their affair in 1949 or 1950. Their relationship had the blessing of her husband Eddie who had his own extracurricular activities, including a

Toni Mannix, Silver Screen Cinema Collection

Japanese American mistress. The Mannixes had a sophisticated European-style "open" marriage.

Reeves called his possessive lover Toni "Mama" or "Mama Toni" while she referred to him as "the boy." Toni was eight years older than Reeves. Toni was mad about her boy, and nothing was too good for him. While Reeves did work, he was still being taken care of by his generous lover. She purchased the Benedict Canyon home for him as well as flashy automobiles and paid his household bills. The money Reeves made himself seems to have been spent on excessive tips, loans to friends, and a movie star's lifestyle on a modest TV star's salary. Reeves was known to tip hundred dollar bills to waiters, people who delivered his liquor, etc. He'd say, "Here's a hundred, kid. Go out and make your first million."

Noel Neill who played Lois Lane on *Superman* said, "He couldn't have possibly had anything left of his meager salary after helping everybody. He was very generous and did a lot of work with children's groups." Jack

Larson remembers that he had a sign over his dressing room door, which read "Honest George—the People's Friend." "I think he gave away as much money as he earned."[57]

For approximately seven years, Reeves and Toni enjoyed a comfortable and happy relationship. Toni's husband approved of his wife's liaison with Reeves and wanted to see her happy. When Toni was content, Eddie, who was twenty-five years older than his wife and suffered from heart disease, could live his life as he chose. It took the pressure of trying to make his wife happy off him. On occasion, Reeves actually stayed in the Mannix home, and Toni spent time at the Benedict Canyon home she purchased for him. The three, all Catholics, would go to Mass together on Sundays.

During the time of their affair, Toni consoled Reeves when his part in *From Here to Eternity* (1953) was drastically cut. It seems preview audiences snickered when Reeves came on the screen, saying, "There's Superman." Reeves was devastated when his part was cut down and felt he'd be trapped as Superman forever.

For years, Toni spoke of a dream house farther up the canyon that she was building for herself and Reeves. He agreed with the idea only if Toni would leave Eddie and marry him. Toni didn't want to do that because she had MGM stock and was tied to her husband financially. Also, Eddie was ill, and her plan was to marry Reeves once Eddie died.

Reeves made the fateful decision to break off the relationship and move on. Toni was distraught at the break-up; in fact she became obsessed and emotionally unstable. She would call Reeves's home at all hours. She just wanted to hear his voice. Reeves would change his phone number, and within a day or two, she'd call again, sometimes up to twenty or thirty times a day. She had taken to following him as well. Finally, Reeves filed a complaint with the Los Angeles District Attorney's office, saying that he believed the caller was Toni Mannix. Today they would call this stalking. At some point, she hired her gardener to make some of the phone calls so they wouldn't be coming from her phone.

---

[57]   Biography, George Reeves: The Perils of a Superhero, February 9, 2000

Reeves then purchased what had to be one of the first telephone answering machines. It was a big reel-to-reel tape recorder. Toni would leave messages, saying things like, "How dare you not be home."[58]

Some say that Toni was also behind the kidnapping of Reeves's pet schnauzer Sam. When Reeves would do errands, he'd bring the dog along, who would ride in the passenger seat. When he returned to the car one day, Sam was gone. An ad was run for the return of the dog, but no one ever responded.

In the months preceding his death, Reeves had two near miss automobile incidents and one accident. His car was almost crushed by two trucks on the freeway. Another time, a speeding car almost killed him. The third accident occurred when Reeves was unable to stop his Jaguar and hit a cement abutment on Benedict Canyon. His head hit the windshield, and he had to have twenty-seven stitches. When the mechanic checking his car took a closer look, he discovered the brake fluid had been drained.

In 1937 Eddie Mannix's first wife Bernice sued him for divorce in California, where she would have been awarded half the community property, and was also requesting $4,000.00 per month in alimony. The car she was riding in with Palm Springs casino owner Al Wertheimer was run off the road. Bernice was killed, and Wertheimer was left crippled.

One theory in this case is that Eddie and Toni Mannix were co-conspirators in the murder of George Reeves. Eddie was tired of seeing his wife so devastated and distraught over the break-up and hired a hit man.

Decades after Reeves's death, Beverly Hills public relations executive Edward Lozzi lived platonically with Toni Mannix. He remembers that she kept a shrine to George Reeves and prayed to him every Tuesday night. There was a picture of Reeves on one side and Jesus on the other. "Toni was terrified of going to hell, so she had me call a priest," says Lozzi, who added that she was completely coherent that day. Toni, who later passed away of complications of Alzheimer's disease, began to confess and bargain with the

---

[58]   Kashner, Sam. *Hollywood Kryptonite: The Bulldog, The Lady, and the Death of Superman*. New York: St. Martin's Press, 1st ed., 1996

priest, asking whether there was a lesser room in hell she'd be sent to if she had orchestrated Reeves's death but didn't actually pull the trigger.[59]

George Reeves left his entire estate to Toni Mannix. She asked Jack Larson to accompany her to the house not long after Reeves's death. He remembered feeling sick when seeing bloody sheets in the bathtub and watching Toni nail prayer cards over the bullet holes.

Larson has defended both Toni and Eddie Mannix against the accusations. He doesn't believe Toni would have done anything to directly hurt Reeves and that Eddie wouldn't have taken the risk. He remembered that Toni absolutely believed that Reeves was murdered. Her theory was that Leonore Lemmon replaced blanks with bullets in the gun, knowing that eventually Reeves would play Russian roulette.

Leonore Lemmon—Suspect

When George Reeves's relationship with Toni Mannix ended, he met an attractive, yet combative, raven-haired beauty in New York—Leonore Lemmon. Lem, as she was known, had a reputation in New York café society as a drunken brawler who had been ejected from both the Stork Club and El Morocco. Lemmon had a violent temper and a volatile personality. She had once punched out another glamour girl at the Stork Club. On another

Leonore Lemmon in 1941 © Corbis.

occasion, she had become furious with a female nightclub photographer, who was wearing a cocktail waitress-style outfit, for cutting her out of a picture. She took her lit cigarette and set the photographer's short skirt on fire. Someone had to dump an ice bucket with champagne over the photographer to put it out.

---

[59] *Extra,* "Edward Lozzi," Syndicated, 1999

Superman Museum curator Jim Hambrick related the following to Geraldo Rivera: "Leonore Lemmon killed George Reeves, and that is a fact. And this is from information compiled by people who were close to her and talked to her at the time. George had broken the news to Lenore that he didn't want to get married. They had argued throughout the course of the day and evening. Leonore was very upset, and George was in the shower. Leonore went upstairs at about twelve thirty in the morning or so. She pulled the Luger out of the side drawer where George kept it. He came out of the shower and tried to wrestle the gun from her. He knocked her down on the floor, and she shot him. Before she went downstairs, she wiped the gun clean, threw it down, picked up a couple of the casings, went downstairs, and told everybody that George had committed suicide. She said she was arguing with him to try and stop him. She pretty much convinced everyone downstairs that was what happened. It took forty-five minutes to call the police.

"One day I was talking to Leonore Lemmon on the phone," continued Hambrick. "We were actually arguing. She told me, 'Do you want to hear that I killed George Reeves?' And I said, 'Only if you did.' 'OK, I killed George Reeves; are you satisfied?' And then she hung up on me."[60]

Author Chuck Harter adds, "What led us to believe that Leonore Lemmon shot him were several things. She lied about the extra bullet holes. She broke the police seal on the house and removed several items. She went to the refrigerator and took all the lunch meat, all the whiskey, and $4,000.00 worth of traveler's checks. When she got to New York, it was discovered that some of the traveler's checks were missing, and there had to have been a burglary of some sort. She immediately turned the checks over to her attorney.

"The funny thing is that when she is intoxicated at the scene of the murder, she tells the police she predicted George going upstairs and shooting himself. The next day when she spoke to columnist Earl Wilson, she said, 'What are you talking about? I never predicted anything.' So again,

---

[60]   *Now it Can Be Told*, Geraldo Rivera (Host), "George Reeves," Cable News Network, 1992

this is another lie on her part. George had made it clear to Leonore that he didn't want to marry her."[61]

Merrill Sparks, who played piano bar at Paul's Steak House in Beverly Hills, recalled that Reeves and Lemmon were arguing the night of the murder. The LAPD never questioned him.

When asked how George Reeves would have liked to have been remembered, Phyllis Coates, the first Lois Lane, said, "Not as Superman but as a decent human being, fun-loving, kind, and generous, which he was." Noel Neill replied, "I'll always remember him as a Southern gentleman. He was so kind and such a gentleman as opposed to so many people in this business." And Jack Larson said, "As honest George, the people's friend."[62]

A much older, bloated Lemmon appeared on *Inside Edition* in 1989 shortly before her death and said in a slurry voice, "I heard a thud, and I did say in all honesty that George is going to shoot himself. I cannot answer you for a million dollars as to why I said that." Becoming the fiery, combative Lem of old, she suddenly exclaimed, "I think he's dead, and the subject is just as dead."

Lemmon was wrong. The subject will never be dead. Reeves has left a legacy of kindness, and as much as he disliked the role, he will be the one and only Superman to an entire generation. And they will always care about what happened that long ago night when it turned out that he was just mortal after all.

---

[61]   *Talk of The Town*, John Craig, Long Beach, California, Public Access, 1992
[62]   Biography, George Reeves: The Perils of a Superhero, February 9, 2000

Chapter 8

The Secret Life of
Bob Crane (1978)

Bob Crane circa 1963, Silver Screen Cinema Collection

The heat was stifling and oppressive, in excess of one hundred degrees, when Victoria Berry, a gorgeous, blonde Australian actress from Bob Crane's play *Beginner's Luck* arrived at the Crane apartment at about two o'clock on Thursday, June 29, 1978, for an appointment. The morning paper was still on the front stoop. She knocked on the door and called for Crane. No one answered. She tried the door, and strangely it was unlocked. Crane always had his door locked and dead-bolted from the inside. She walked from the bright, blazing Arizona sun into the darkened, air-conditioned apartment.

"It was dark, really dark," Victoria Berry Welles remembered in a 1998 interview with *E! True Hollywood Story*. "All the drapes were closed." Welles saw a body in a fetal position on the bed. Blood was pooled around the head, and at first she thought it might be Crane's friend John Carpenter (who had long black hair) or possibly a woman. She went a little closer and saw the expensive French wrist watch. "I wouldn't admit to myself that it was Bob Crane. I was in the *Twilight Zone*. It was like I was on another planet. I couldn't even cry." Ed Beck, Windmill Theater executive, later made final identification of the body. "There is no way I would have been able to identify him from one side. The other side…yes."[63]

Crane's bed and pillowcases were soaked with blood. Blood splatter and tissue were on the walls and pillowcases. A cord from a video camera was cut and reportedly tied in a bow around his neck. Although crime scene photos don't show the bow, the chief medical examiner, Dr. Heinz Karnitsching, said Crane thankfully never knew what hit him. "I decided then and there that ligature was not instrumental in causing his death. The man had obviously been struck with a blunt instrument over the left temple."

There were no signs of a break-in. The apartment was cluttered with videotapes and Polaroid pictures of Crane, along with his friend John Carpenter, each engaged in sexual activity with various women, sometimes two or three at a time.

---

[63] The majority of interview quotes from this chapter are from the documentaries *Murder in Scottsdale, A & E Biography* and *E! True Hollywood Story*. Please see bibliography.

Crime Scene Photo—Crane's Videos and Video Tape Recorder,
Crime Scene Photo

There was even a makeshift darkroom in the bathroom where Crane would develop film of his sexual encounters. A camera was also pointed toward the couch, where it's been said Crane filmed seductions of women without their knowledge. Carpenter traveled for his video business and would follow Crane's play *Beginner's Luck* from town to town so they could party and get women. Crane would get first choice and Carpenter the remainder of the women.

In the documentary *Murder in Scottsdale* (2003), which is a special feature on the *Auto Focus* (2001) DVD (a film about Bob Crane starring Greg Kinnear), Detective Jim Raines spoke of the missing murder weapon.

Detective Raines was brought in during the second investigation of the case in 1990 by the Maricopa County Attorney's Office. "At the time of the homicide, the murder weapon was unknown. When I observed the sheets from the bed from the Scottsdale evidence room, I observed two marks on the sheets. I noticed it was a *V* shape. I suspected possibly a tripod at that point."

From photographs of Crane's apartment, Detective Raines noticed that a tripod was missing from the crime scene. He went out and purchased a similar tripod and took it to a forensic expert. "He had the sheet spread out on the table and the tripod on top of it. It was an absolute perfect match. Not only did the legs match, but the head of the tripod actually matched the wound," explained Raines.

There were things in the apartment that shouldn't have been there, and other items were missing. Crane, who was just a couple of weeks away from turning fifty at the time of his death, was a teetotaler and yet there was whiskey and beer in the apartment. The autopsy reports that no alcohol or drugs were found in Crane's system. There were cigarettes (Crane didn't smoke), and a photo album (one of many) containing sex pictures of Crane with various women was missing, as were some of the videos.

By the front door were his friend Carpenter's swimming trunks and an edited video (with curse words cut out) of *Saturday Night Fever* which Carpenter was supposed to take with him to Los Angeles, for Crane's young son Scotty. Crane had noted in his date book that he was to drive Carpenter to the airport the day of his murder. Well over thirty years later, many questions regarding Crane's murder remain unanswered, and the case remains officially unsolved.

Bob Crane

Robert Edward Crane was born in Waterbury, Connecticut, in 1928, the younger of two sons, to Alfred and Rosemary Crane. As a young boy, he was a class clown who started playing drums at the age of eight. By the time he was fourteen, Crane was playing drums for the Connecticut Symphony Orchestra. He met his first wife, Anne Terzian, in the Stamford High School marching band. He would marry his high school sweetheart in 1950 after serving in the National Guard. With his first wife, Anne, he had three children: Robert David, born in 1951; Deborah Ann, born in 1959; and Karen Leslie, born in 1961.

*The Crane Family: Robert David Crane (top), Bob
Crane, Debbie, Karen, and his first wife Ann—Silver
Screen Cinema Collection*

His oldest son Robert recalled to A & E Biography, "My dad's heroes were Buddy Rich, Louis Belson, and Gene Krupa. That was what he wanted to do. He wanted to be in a big band and drum and hit the road. At the age of fourteen, he was with the Connecticut Symphony Orchestra. Two years later they fired him for not being serious enough."

Following five years of being a professional drummer, Crane obtained his first radio job. In a 1972 interview with Chicago radio station WCFL, Crane recollected, "Once I got into radio, the man who hired me said everything I did was funny, including the news. So he said, 'You just be the funny guy with the records.' That's how I got into the comedy end of it. My main ambition was to get to New York City. I thought that I could turn this into acting. What I was doing on radio was creating an image."

The career game-changing phone call Crane received was not from New York but from Los Angeles radio station KNX, which was in the CBS family. He signed a five-year contract with KNX, where he quickly became known as "King of the Airwaves" and was earning a six-figure salary. Soon he was being offered television talk shows. His comedy was often compared to that of Steve Allen. He was then offered game show host jobs, such as replacing Johnny Carson on *Who Do You Trust?*, and hosting an updated *This Is Your Life*. Crane turned all these offers down. He had his heart set on being an actor.

Gary Owens of *Laugh-In* fame once said, "Bob told me many times when we would have breakfast or lunch together, that he wanted to be the next Jack Lemmon. He felt that Jack was the epitome of being a comedic actor."

Los Angeles radio and TV personality Tom Hatten remembered that he and Crane did local theater during their years on radio, hoping to catch the attention of studio talent scouts and prove that they could act.

Crane remembered that he always liked the buddy part because it was almost always the comedy role. "I always played the swinging next door neighbor. About that time I did *The Dick Van Dyke Show*. Up until that time I was doing one or two line bits on television. I was always the guy who said, 'Come on…let's get a bunch of girls and have a party.' I did a good role on *The Dick Van Dyke Show* and *The Donna Reed Show* and people saw it. They said, 'Hey, we thought the reason you weren't doing television was because you had two heads and a long tail or something. You're not bad-looking. You do comedy well. How would you like to do our show?'" Crane was on *The Donna Reed Show* from 1963 to 1965.

There are differing opinions as to why Crane left *The Donna Reed Show*. Some say he was fired. Others say it was because of a salary dispute. Crane himself said it was illness. At the time he was on the program, Crane was still working on his radio show in the early mornings, leaving at ten o'clock in the morning for the Donna Reed set. It was a hectic schedule. "I was earning as I was learning," Crane once explained.

Paul Petersen, who played Reed's son Jeff on the show, has said, "The only disturbing element right from the beginning was his attitude toward Donna and his treatment of Ann McCrea, who played his wife, which was far too cozy, touchy, feely, right from the get-go."

While Petersen may have noticed that Crane had an over-familiarity with women, other colleagues noticed just the opposite.

KNX Executive Tom Bernstein remembered being at a strip club following a board meeting after Crane left the radio station, during the time when *Hogan's Heroes* aired. He was shocked when Crane came into the place and that he knew all the girls. "I remembered Bob as a 'Mr. Straight Arrow' kind of guy."

Crane drove a station wagon, not an expensive car, didn't smoke, rarely drank, and used to play volleyball a couple of times a week at the YMCA with Art Linkletter. He didn't have a house in Beverly Hills but rather in Tarzana, a suburb of the San Fernando Valley. He was a practicing Catholic who went to church most Sundays.

Soon after leaving *The Donna Reed Show,* Crane was presented a script for a show entitled *Heroes.* It was later changed to *Hogan's Heroes.* Colonel Robert Hogan is the role for which Crane will always be best remembered. He received two Emmy nominations for his portrayal of the Colonel who headed a disorderly group of Allied officers in a German prisoner of war camp. Week after week, the Allies outwitted the bumbling Nazis.

When the show was first on the air, it endured some controversy, as many people thought it took place in a concentration camp rather than a POW camp. Ironically, several of the show's co-stars, Robert Clary (Corporal LeBeau), John Banner (Sergeant Schultz), and Leon Askin (General Burkhalter) were held in concentration or internment camps during World War II. Werner Klemperer (Colonel Klink) fled Nazi Germany in 1933. Klemperer said, "If I can play Richard III, then I can play a Nazi." He also insisted Hogan win over the Germans in every instance, or he wouldn't do the series. And Banner once asked, "Who can play Nazis better than us Jews?"

Crane, handsome with almond-shaped dark brown eyes, a twinkle in his eye, and a warm, friendly smile, had a high TVQ (TV star popularity rating) . He was well liked by just about everyone. *Hogan's Heroes* was a highly rated and popular program from 1965 to 1971. This time Crane gave up his day job as a disc jockey at KNX Radio and devoted himself completely to the hit TV series.

"I prefer comedy because it actually comes easier to me," explained Crane in a 1971 Drury Theater interview. "I'm actually a cut-up, and I always was. I like people who have a sense of humor. I hate people who take themselves seriously. I like to watch drama, and I'd love to do it someday. I feel my strong point is comedy."

It was during his time on *Hogan's Heroes* that Crane's personality began to noticeably change. The once happily married "straight arrow" seemed to get a somewhat inflated ego with his newfound success and started taking advantage of opportunities where women were concerned. After filming all day, Crane began playing drums in strip clubs and topless and bottomless bars.

Through his *Hogan's Heroes* co-star Richard Dawson, Crane was introduced to John Carpenter, a video equipment salesman. Crane had always enjoyed splicing audiotapes and creating comedy routines for his radio show. He became fascinated with videotaped home movies and editing them.

The still-married Crane began an affair with his married co-star Cynthia Lynn, who portrayed Col. Klink's secretary Helga during the first season of *Hogan's Heroes*. "I was falling in love with him and he with me," said

Bob Crane and second wife Sigrid Valdis on the set of Hogan's Heroes © CBS Television. Silver Screen Cinema Collection

Lynn. "We were planning on marriage. Nobody knew about it. It was between him and me. Anyway we were close, very close." Lynn decided to work things out with her husband, and the affair ended.

Crane's co-star Werner Klemperer noted, "I would say Bob enjoyed females. And I don't think he was the most discreet person."

The next actress to come in and play Klink's secretary was Patti Olson (stage name Sigrid Valdis). Again Crane began an affair with a co-star. Shortly after his divorce from Terzian, Crane married Olson on the set of *Hogan's Heroes* in 1970, which co-star Robert Clary found odd. He wondered why they'd marry on the set rather than in a church. In 1971 Crane and Olson had a son, Robert Scott, known as Scotty.

Although he was married for the second time, Crane's sexual obsessions did not end. He began to videotape and photograph his encounters with the help of his friend Carpenter who shared the same fixations and also reaped the benefit of getting women through the handsome actor.

Olson knew of her husband's sexual proclivities. In 2006 she told ABC News (*20/20*), "He didn't lose his first amendment rights when he married me—he loved having sex and filming it. He never broke any laws. Nothing he did was unconstitutional."

When asked whether she was envious of the women Crane was having sex with, Olson replied, "No. Bob used these women. He said, 'I wish when I was finished with them I could just push a button, and they'd fall through the floor and disappear.' Now how could I be jealous of something like that? He treated women like the rest of the world treats toilet paper. Who's going to be jealous of that?" Olson passed away from lung cancer one year after the interview with *20/20*.

Following the cancellation of *Hogan's Heroes,* Crane did guest spots on *Police Woman, Gibbsville, Night Gallery*, and *Love American Style,* among other television shows. He also had his own series in 1975, *The Bob Crane Show*, which lasted for only thirteen episodes and was severely condemned by the critics.

With the Disney film *Superdad* (1974), Crane had a chance to become the big screen star he had always dreamed of being. When the film was about

Angie Dickinson and Bob Crane in a 1974 episode of Police Woman © NBC Television, Silver Screen Cinema Collection

to be released, rumors of Crane's secret private life began to surface. Disney distanced itself from the actor.

Crane bought the rights to a play entitled *Beginner's Luck* and took it on the road. His friend Carpenter would make business trips to coincide with the cities and states where Crane's play would run.

"I like working with a live audience," said Crane. "I prefer that over working to just a camera where there's nobody that's responding. You tell a joke, and nothing happens. On stage you tell a joke, and you hear the laughter or you don't. And if you don't, you begin analyzing in your mind…why didn't I? Either I delivered it wrong, or I was standing wrong. Or the audience didn't hear it. There's always a reason why."

The Days Prior to the Murder and Little Known Theories

Victoria Berry Welles, the actress who discovered Crane's body, remembered driving through Scottsdale with Crane and feeling a sense of foreboding. "I remember him saying to me, 'This town is loaded, known for the mob.' It was a haunting feeling, it was the way he said it. And he said it more than once." There were rumors of jealous husbands and boyfriends of the women whom Crane dallied with, wanting revenge.

Robert Graysmith, author of *The Murder of Bob Crane* and *Auto Focus*, told of an incident with Crane's car just before his death. It was pitch black, and Crane was in the parking lot of the Windmill Theater following a performance of his play. "His car doesn't start," says Graysmith. "Now later they look at his tire, and the valve core has been tampered with. Somebody was trying to strand him in that parking lot. He and John Carpenter were there. But Bob, one of the things that make him delightful, is that he is unpredictable. He gets into his car. He takes off for the lights of the far away service station, riding on the rim of the flat tire. The service guy at the station is looking at it and realizes it's been tampered with. And that station attendant actually took that tire, replaced it, and kept the old tire. He was going to show it to the police. He thought something was really up. I think so too. I think it was a warning for Bob Crane."[64]

Also the night before the homicide, Crane was reported to have had an argument on the phone with his wife Olson. The couple was going through a bitter divorce, and she had accused Crane of showing his homemade pornography tapes to his young son Scotty. Crane vehemently denied this. Police Lt. Barry Vassall has said that phone tolls showed Crane called his wife in Bainbridge Island, Washington. All airline flights were checked and there were no flights that would have allowed her to be in Arizona at the time of the murder.

A motorcyclist told police that he saw a blonde woman leaving Crane's apartment, carrying a long object in butcher paper. The motorcyclist had been drinking, and police dismissed the story.

At four o'clock on the morning of Crane's murder, there was a moving van with three movers. This is the only cool time of day to do heavy work, like moving in the scorching heat of summer in Scottsdale.

Police Lt. Vassall said they always knew there were movers but didn't know who they were. Years after the homicide, one of the movers called the Scottsdale Police Department and spoke to Vassall.

"He told me that he and his friend were loading furniture. He saw a female, whom he described as good-looking. She walked through the parking lot and went into Crane's apartment. Within a matter of seconds or minutes, she left the apartment screaming hysterically. He said he thought he saw a man come out of the same apartment. I think the killer was trapped in the apartment waiting for the movers to leave. There was blood on the curtain of the front window. The man left in a white car and matched the description of John Carpenter."

---

[64]   Graysmith, Robert. *The Murder of Bob Crane*. New York, NY: Crown, 1993.

*Gig Young and Bob Crane in an episode of
Gibbsville (1974) © NBC Television—
Silver Screen Cinema Collection*

It seemed as though the worse Crane's career was going, the more aggressively he pursued women and his sexual obsessions. He would show his photo albums with pornographic pictures to just about anyone who came to visit him. It seemed to be an ego boost, a form of validation for him.

Crane's oldest son Robert says, "I've heard many things over the years: mob hit, jealous boyfriend, jealous husband, drugs; I ruled all that out because, first of all, there was no break-in to the apartment where my dad was staying. There was no struggle. There was no robbery except for a photograph book. And the scene was left pretty much without turmoil, is how I kind of gauge it. He was asleep. He looked comfortable…you know in his bed…no struggle. So, I'm thinking back now, this is someone that he knows. The door's unlocked. A couple of scenarios, he either lets the person in at the front door and feels comfortable enough to go in his bedroom and go to sleep. He leaves the door unlocked for a person he feels comfortable with, or the person who came over had a key."

John Carpenter—Suspect

On June 27, two days before Crane was found dead, he and Carpenter were at Bobby McGee's nightclub/restaurant. Waitress Linda Davis remembers the two men discussing something that both seemed upset about. The discussion was not at all friendly.

Detective Jim Raines reported that witnesses had testified that they also saw the two men argue at the Safari restaurant the night before Crane's death. This was the last time Crane was seen alive. One witness said that Carpenter acted like a hurt lover. While photographs and tapes showed no evidence of a homosexual relationship between Carpenter and Crane, Crane's oldest son Robert has said that there was another tape that showed Carpenter in a sexual encounter with a well-known male entertainer.

Crane's autopsy report states that he was wearing just white boxer shorts and that there was a flaky, white dry material in the pubic hair, right lower abdomen, and right interior thigh.

Police Sergeant Dennis Borkenhagen recalled, "There appeared to be semen on his right thigh. But at autopsy it was still there. I asked if they would collect the semen, and the medical examiner investigator said, 'What's that going to tell you except that he had a piece of ass.'" What the medical examiner investigator didn't think of is that it might not have been Crane's semen at all. The semen could have belonged to the killer.

Sergeant Borkenhagen recalled questioning Carpenter shortly after the murder and that Carpenter said, "Remind me about urination." Following his questioning he asked Carpenter about urination. Carpenter said that Crane always urinated immediately after sex because he thought it lessened the chance of getting sexually transmitted diseases such as VD. "And to me that was almost an admission," says Borkenhagen. "Why would he think that would be important to us unless he knew there was semen on Crane's leg?"

Police and others have theorized that the video cord found around Crane's neck was symbolic of the severing of a relationship. Police also thought that the missing photograph album was a red herring to throw suspicion on a jealous husband or boyfriend who may have stolen the album to get incriminating pictures. Police wondered how Carpenter would know the album wasn't there unless he took it.

Crane told his oldest son Robert, "'The situation with Carpenter had become a pain in the ass.' My dad said, 'It used to be fun, we'd hang out together, go to clubs, that kind of thing. Now it's become a hanger-on situation.'"

Detective Jim Raines pointed out, "This is a thirteen-year friendship that has ended. John Carpenter will not get the residual women. He will not get the drinks, the party life."

Carpenter did not take the end of his friendship with Crane lightly. Carpenter left two and a half hours early for the airport on the morning of June 29. He told police he called Crane at three o'clock in the morning and told him that he would take himself to the airport. Lt. Dean said, "I believe he went to the apartment at three o'clock in the morning, not this phone call he described to us."

Carpenter took his white rental car back, complaining of a problem with the electrical system and requested that the car be cleaned and detailed.

Lt. Ron Dean remembers that Carpenter called Crane's apartment three times during a two-hour period after Crane's body was discovered. Dean said he identified himself as police, and never once did Carpenter ask why the police were in his best friend's apartment, which Dean thought was strange. It was almost like a criminal returning to the scene of the crime.

Carpenter also called Crane's son Robert and told him to call him if he needed anything. This was before the news of Crane's death had been made public. Robert said, "He called the Windmill Theater, he called me, he called the apartment. I always thought this is the kind of thing a guilty person would do. You are going to want to place yourself in California."

Police impounded Carpenter's rental car. Blood smears were found on the door panels, window toggle switch, and the passenger side of the car. Some blood transfers were as long as six inches in length. There was also blood on the doorknob leading outside from the apartment.

There was no DNA profiling in 1978; however, the blood was typed and matched Crane's Type B, which is present in only 10 percent of the population.

Police were frustrated because they were told that unless they had fingerprints on a murder weapon or a confession the DA wouldn't prosecute. The district attorney at the time, Charles Hyder, felt there wasn't enough blood and that because it was a rental car there was no evidence to show how long it had been there.

So the Crane murder case remained cold for well over a decade. A new Maricopa County district attorney, Richard Romley, reopened the case in 1990. Romley said that the Scottsdale Police Department wanted the case to be reviewed. They believed they did not get a fair shot at presenting all the evidence to an unbiased county attorney.

"With the advent of DNA and new technologies that might help us, I said OK, let's see what we have," explained Romley.

The case was re-investigated just as though the homicide had just occurred. Detective Raines found a photograph that he felt was a smoking gun to this case. A previous county investigator had placed a photograph of blood tissue in a notebook. This tissue photographed was inside of Carpenter's car. Raines took the photograph to five pathologists to render an opinion of what the substance was. No background was given to the pathologists as to what this might be. Each said it was subcutaneous tissue. And one of the pathologists noticed a hair coming out of it. This photo of the tissue matched photos of the tissue found on Crane's pillow.

Unfortunately, the tissue sample was lost. Detective Raines said, "To me the tissue inside the car was an extension of the murder scene. The only way that the tissue would get from the murder scene to the car was to be carried by someone."

Bob Crane Defendant John Henry Carpenter talks with his attorney Gary Fleischman in a Los Angeles courtroom, CA, June 1, 1992 (AP Photo/Douglas C. Pizac)

District Attorney Romley said, "We had blood inside the car, and the blood type matched Bob Crane's. We had the photograph that appeared very similar to the types of tissue found from the bloody crime scene, which was found on the pillow case. All of those things together, we thought were going to convince a jury."

Since Carpenter was in California, a fugitive warrant was issued for Carpenter's arrest. He called his wife and said, "They finally got me. I'm under arrest." He told Mark Dawson, son of Richard Dawson, that he did not kill his best friend.

Carpenter's trial was delayed for two years because he was being held in California for sexual misconduct with a minor. The trial of John Henry Carpenter lasted three days. On October 31, 1994, Carpenter was found not guilty of the murder of Bob Crane.

It seems a picture of the tissue wasn't considered the same as the actual tissue to the jury. Jurors who were interviewed felt the evidence was circumstantial. They also didn't care about the sex tape that was shown to them. They felt the tape was the participants' own private business. If actual DNA had been found, it would have been different, said one juror. The blood samples were not properly preserved and had lessened with each testing over the years.

Four years after the trial ended, Carpenter died of a heart attack at the age of seventy-two. Mark Dawson felt that being under scrutiny for so many years and the trial itself took a toll on Carpenter. Dawson said that Carpenter was ruined after the trial.

Had he not had a sexual addiction and been killed at such a young age, there's no telling where Crane's career would have taken him. He was a natural performer and a great, likable comedic actor. Another Jack Lemmon? Very possibly.

Crane's children from his two families have been divided for decades. In 1975 Crane added a codicil to his will, in effect disinheriting the three older children from his first marriage. He left them $5,000.00 each, and the remainder of his estate went to his second family. Also, Robert Crane and Scotty Crane fought bitterly over the portrayal of their father in the 2001 film *Auto Focus.*

Author Robert Graysmith says that Crane thought he was broke. Unbeknownst to Crane, his business manager Lloyd Vaughn had embezzled $100,000.00 from him. Crane also had no idea how valuable the percentage he owned in *Hogan's Heroes* would have become. Had he lived, by 1990 Crane would have had 25 percent of $90 million. His other co-stars only got paid for the first six syndicated appearances.

His middle daughter Debbie remembers, "When he was at home, he was a perfectly normal father like the man down the street. You could not tell the difference. My father was a wonderful father. He was very doting, very protective, very loving."

His son Robert says, "Ninety percent of my dad is really Hogan, the all-American good guy, trying to do the best that he can. Ten percent is that dark, quirky, closet side."

His youngest daughter Karen explains, "My dad was the guy next door. He was everyone's friend, had a quick wit, and was always happy. The man we knew was not the man on those tabloids."

At the time of this writing, his youngest son Scotty, a radio personality and actor himself, has started a campaign to get his father in the National Radio Hall of Fame. After all, he was in radio long before he was an actor. And Crane was an innovator in the field. He actually had to take a pay cut from his radio salary to star on *Hogan's Heroes*.

Ed Beck, a minister as well as Windmill Theater executive, had been counseling Crane shortly before his death. "He did not like that this addiction controlled him. If Bob Crane had not been murdered, I definitely think he would have changed. And his motivation for change would have been his family. He did not want his children to grow up and look at him in a negative light. He loved the father role. He loved what he understood a good father to be."

At least that is one wish Crane achieved. His children think very highly of him. His son Robert says, "I guess above all, I always think about the waste. So needless...so unnecessary...so wasteful. He should be here."

CHAPTER 9

Gig Young–Game of Death (1978)

Gig Young as he appeared in Tell it to the Judge
(1949) © Columbia Pictures—Silver Screen
Cinema Collection

At the Osborne, one of the first luxury apartment houses in New York City, on a crisp, fall Thursday afternoon in 1978, apartment manager Constas Mastsoukas thought he heard a noise…possibly a car backfiring, or maybe it was the window gutting he ordered for the building. He went back to his lunch, not thinking too much about it. A few hours later, he saw two bags of groceries containing perishables, which had been delivered earlier, sitting outside the front door of Suite 1BB.

As the day wore on, Matsoukas checked with the doorman who claimed that the residents of apartment IBB, Academy Award ®-winning actor Gig Young and Kim, his young bride of just three weeks, had not left the building nor had they had any visitors. The manager tried calling the couple on the house phone, never getting an answer. With the groceries still by the front of the door by early evening, Mastsoukas began to worry that perhaps it wasn't a car backfiring or windows being gutted that he had heard, and reluctant to use his passkey, called the police.

Gig and Kim Young in 1977 © Ron Gallela/Getty Images

The apartment was dimly lit and eerily quiet when the police entered. Two fully clothed bodies, which lay opposite each other, were on the floor in the bathroom. The blonde, thirty-one-year-old woman all dressed up with jewelry, expensive brown leather boots, a green velour blouse, and gray slacks lay on her back. One earring was on her ear and the other was under her body. Blood was pooled around her head, matting her blonde hair. The man, age sixty-four, was lying face down in the blood-soaked carpet. His necktie was loose; he hadn't gotten around to knotting it. Still gripped in his hand was a .38 caliber Smith and Wesson. It appeared Gig Young had shot himself in the mouth, "sucking the gun," as Homicide Lieutenant Richard Gallagher called it, after allegedly shooting his wife Kim in the base of the skull.

There were at least three firearms in the apartment as well as 350 rounds of ammunition in dresser drawers, yet Young's friends later insisted that he hated guns and was afraid to fire them even with blanks in films. There was no suicide note; however, a blood-splattered diary on the desk was open to September 27, with the notation, "We got married today." For nearly four decades, people have been wondering why?

Young's agent Martin Baum once said, "He seemed like a man who had everything going for him. How little we know."

It was an incongruous ending for the actor who most remember as a handsome, amiable sophisticate. The image of Young of countless films with his smashing good looks and perennial twinkle in his eye, impeccably dressed, sipping a martini, and sporting a crooked smile comes to mind. Whether it was Cary Grant, Frank Sinatra, or Clark Gable, he almost always lost the girl to the leading man by the fadeout of the movie. In an interview the year of his death, Young said that the "second fiddle" roles "took a toll on my personal happiness. You lose self-confidence in the real life as opposed to the reel life. Even though this might not make sense to many people, you play a loser long enough, and you end up a loser—at least you are convinced you are a loser."[65]

Gig Young was born Byron Elsworth Barr in St. Cloud, Minnesota, in 1913. He was a sickly, middle child who felt overshadowed by his older brother Don and his beloved little sister Genevieve. The family owned a cannery and was very well off for most of Young's upbringing. Following the Depression, the family's fortunes took a turn for the worse.

The definitive 1991 Young biography *Final Gig* by the late George Eells reveals Young's insecurities as a child that would later become demons as an adult. Eells heard much of this posthumously from the actor himself in a collection of autobiographical/analytical audiotapes Young left behind.

---

[65] Buckley, Michael. "Gig Young: Were Life Simpler than It Is He'd Have Fared Better," *Films in Review*, February 1971.

It seems his parents were cold to him, ignoring him in favor of his siblings. His mother had emotional problems herself and was prone to depression. She left the day-to-day raising of her child to a distant relative, Aunt Jesse, who at age seventeen came to stay with the family and act as a nanny. This nanny began to sexually abuse Young as well as emotionally taunt him by showering him with affection and then inexplicably taking it away. This abuse was to color his relationships for the remainder of his life with women who were either substitute mother figures or glamorous, young actresses.

Young, who always had a love for acting, beginning with high school plays and amateur groups, eventually earned a scholarship to the Pasadena Community Playhouse. A Warner Brothers talent scout signed both Young and George Reeves on the same day after seeing them in a play in the late 1930s. One of the first parts he was noted for critically was in *The Gay Sisters* (1942). At Warner Brothers' request, Byron Barr took the name of his character in that film, Gig Young, professionally.

Young was riding high at Warner Brothers with films such as *Old Acquaintance* and *Air Force* that were released in 1943. However, he left the studio enlisting in the coast guard during World War II as a pharmacist's mate. During the war Young suffered an injury to the groin area. To relieve the constant swelling from a tubular mass at the back of the testicles, he underwent a vasectomy.

Following his return from the Coast Guard, Young found he had lost the career momentum he had before the War. Warner Brothers let his option go. This was a great blow to Young as he was a company man and loved working for Warner Brothers. He began to freelance, eventually ending up at Columbia making the films he was best known for—sophisticated comedies. Young once said, "Comedy is harder than drama, since comedy roles involve the offbeat, not merely the basic, emotions. I like to play both comedy and drama."

James Cagney and Gig Young in Come Fill the Cup (1951)
© Warner Bros.—Silver Screen Cinema Collection

Young was nominated for an Academy Award ® three times, first for the dramatic *Come Fill the Cup* (1951) with James Cagney and Phyllis Thaxter. Young gave a sterling performance as the alcoholic composer. This film showcased his dramatic talent, particularly the scenes where his character was going through alcohol withdrawal. It was a harbinger of the definitive role of his career in *They Shoot Horses Don't They* almost twenty years later, for which he would win the Oscar ® for Best Supporting Actor as the cynical, cruel master of ceremonies of a dance marathon. He was also nominated for his supporting role as the "too perfect" professor in *Teacher's Pet* (1958) who gets knocked down a peg or two after Gable's character gets him drunk. His combination of an adversarial-buddy on-screen chemistry with Clark Gable, particularly in the "hangover" scene, was faultless.

Clark Gable and Gig Young in Teacher's Pet (1958) ©
Paramount Pictures—Silver Screen Cinema Collection

Young married five times. His first wife was Sheila Stapler, a fellow player at the Pasadena Playhouse; the second, Sophie Rosenstein, was a drama coach with a master's degree from the University of Washington. Their affair began while both were married to others. Following their respective divorces, they married. His marriage to Rosenstein was to last just two years until her death from cancer in 1952. During his wife's illness, they handled the inevitable by pretending nothing was wrong. Young instructed the doctors not tell his wife of her grim prognosis, and she, in turn, pretended not to know. Young was devastated when he lost his wife. Rosenstein gave him confidence and helped direct his career, and he had loved her for years before their short marriage.

Actress Jayne Meadows told author George Eells, "I always thought Sophie was a mother figure to him. He had all the self-confidence of an abused, frightened child. I think that's why he drank, to dull the pain and insecurity. But now there was Sophie to say, 'Little boy, you're handsome.

You're sexy. You're talented.' I'm not saying he was aware of it, but in my opinion, that's why he loved her."[66]

It was during his marriage to Rosenstein that he made the film *Come Fill The Cup*, his greatest role to date and a part she helped him get. Fortunately, Rosenstein lived long enough to attend the Academy Award ® ceremony with her husband. Young lost to Karl Malden for his performance in *A Streetcar Named Desire,* which was something the couple anticipated.

A serious love affair with Elaine Stritch followed his ill-fated marriage to Rosenstein. Her strict Catholicism and the fact that Young had been baptized a Presbyterian and couldn't marry in the Catholic Church, torpedoed their plans for marriage. Yet their friendship endured throughout Young's life.

In 1955 Young was set up on a studio date with gorgeous, impish Elizabeth Montgomery who later achieved fame on television's *Bewitched.* Young was twenty years older than Montgomery, who was at that time co-starring with Gary Cooper in *The Court Marital of Billy Mitchell.* Montgomery had a crush on the actor and was tremendously excited about the date and would often say, "I think he's the most attractive man on the screen, and I intend to marry him."[67]

Young was captivated by her beauty and social grace. She also had an impeccable Hollywood pedigree as the daughter of Robert Montgomery. Montgomery wanted children, and Young had had a

Gig Young and third wife Elizabeth Montgomery, Historical Editorial Archive

---

[66] Eells, George. *Final Gig, The Man Behind the Murder.* Orlando, FL: Harcourt, 1st ed., 1991.

[67] Eells, George. *Final Gig, The Man Behind the Murder.* Orlando, FL: Harcourt, 1st ed., 1991.

vasectomy during the war. Montgomery, then just twenty-three, was willing to overlook this, saying that they would raise dogs instead. Reportedly, Young underwent an operation to reverse his vasectomy.

The couple never did have children. They had many pets, including a lamb named Mary Chess. In the beginning of their marriage, they were described as a delightful couple and very much in love.

Young never got along with his father-in-law, and Montgomery felt overshadowed by her husband's enduring love of his dead wife whose pictures Young kept hidden in a drawer. Young and Montgomery's marriage ended in 1963 amid heavy drinking, allegations of affairs on both sides, and violent arguments.

Young quickly rebounded into a relationship with voluptuous real estate agent to the stars Elaine Garber Whitman, whom he met while looking for a new house after his divorce from Montgomery.

In her 1979 book, *A Million Dollars Down*, Whitman remembered Young as an insecure loner and says his heavy drinking ended their relationship. Although she says he attended Alcoholics Anonymous at the beginning of their marriage, he went back to drinking, or as she put it, he was always "one drink away from doom."

Whitman gave birth to a daughter Jennifer during her marriage to Young, who had decided for a brief time his vasectomy reversal must have worked. Following their acrimonious divorce, Young disputed paternity of the child. However, since he had acknowledged paternity, the courts ruled in favor of Whitman, stating that Young was the father of the child. He never saw Jennifer again following the divorce.

Jennifer, who was fourteen years old at the time of her father's death, has said that she believed it was an accident. She believes that he accidentally shot his bride, and unable to live with what he had done, turned the gun on himself.[68]

Today a writer and singer, Jennifer is at the time of this writing working on a documentary and book entitled *Between a Father and Daughter*.

---

[68]   Lisa, Sophie, Jewel, Tatiana, and Jennifer, as told to Joanne Parrent with Bruce W. Cook. .Los Angeles, CA: Dove Books. *Once More with Feeling—You'll Never Make Love in this Town Again*. 1996.

Whitman, who passed away in 2006, wrote that she also believed it wasn't planned. Both mother and daughter believe the accident occurred under the influence of alcohol; however, Young's autopsy revealed that there were no barbiturates or alcohol in his system. Because of his well-documented issues with alcohol and depression, for decades the public has assumed it was what it appeared to be—an alcohol-fueled murder-suicide. Yet there was no alcohol in his blood. Was Young going through withdrawal? Or was it a tragic accident, and realizing what he had done, Young killed himself? There is another theory that has been largely ignored over the years. Was it murder?

While in the process of divorcing Elaine Whitman in 1967, Young was appearing on Broadway in *There's a Girl in My Soup*. Across the street, *Cactus Flower* was running, featuring twenty-two-year-old Skye Aubrey, daughter of his *Come Fill the Cup* co-star Phyllis Thaxter and James Aubrey, head of CBS and later, MGM.

Reminiscent of Elizabeth Montgomery's crush a decade earlier, Skye Aubrey, a beautiful young woman with an appealing, slightly husky voice and a lovely face faintly sprinkled with freckles, made up her mind that she was going to make Gig Young fall in love with her.

"It's the only time I ever went in pursuit of a man," she explained to this author during our interview. "Gig was always charming and delightful and had a great sense of humor. I trapped him into dating me. I don't know if he would have given me a second look if I hadn't pursued him.

Publicity photo of Gig Young's girlfriend Skye Aubrey during the early 1970s— Silver Screen Cinema Collection

I'm sure the same thing later happened with the girl—Kim. Bob Webber (an actor friend of Young and Aubrey) told me she went after him. Bob couldn't stand the girl. He thought from the beginning that she was wrong for Gig."[69]

Aubrey says that at first her relationship with Young was sexually intense, but later Young suffered bouts of impotence. She kept her own apartment for appearances' sake because of the bitter divorce with Whitman, but she actually lived with Young for one year.

"He was very upset over the divorce and paternity case. It was very messy. Gig was a very nice man but…susceptible," explained Aubrey. "He married Elaine to be nice. It upset me that he deserted the little girl, Jennifer. Even if he thought he wasn't her biological father, he should have accepted paternity."

Regarding the physical relationship between the fifty-four-year-old Young and herself, Aubrey related, "Gig was a 'safety.' Most of the time he was too drunk to have sex. But I was just twenty-two…and that was OK with me. It didn't matter. I felt safe with him. Gig was very protective of me, and I always loved older men. He was very special.

"I used to do a terrible thing to him. When I was twenty-two I looked fifteen. If we had to meet with people from the agency, he'd say, 'Please, Skye darling, don't look fifteen.' I would dress in knee socks, high heels, and a mini-skirt," Aubrey laughed. "It would drive him crazy because he was self-conscious about our age difference."

Aubrey's mother, actress Phyllis Thaxter, was horrified and embarrassed by her young daughter's affair with her one-time leading man. "My mother found the relationship unacceptable. I remember we all had dinner at Sardis—my mother, Gig, and me. It was very awkward."

Asked how she thought Young had changed in the decade or so that she knew him, Aubrey replied, "As he got older, he wanted to stop drinking, and he did. That surprised me. He was suffering from health problems; his teeth, back, and feet were bad, and he had a lot of pain. He was on painkillers.

---

[69]   All Skye Aubrey quotes from interview with author in August 2012.

"One time I went with him when he was on the Johnny Carson show. We were in the green room, and everyone was drinking around him, but Gig didn't drink. I swear he got a contact high from the room because he looked drunk on the program. He never went on that show again."

Another thing Aubrey remembered was that during the years that Young did drink, he never did so while working. "He was very disciplined and would wait until shooting stopped."

When their affair ended, Aubrey remained dear friends with Young. They talked once a month, and he even visited her in London when her daughter was born.

"We remained close friends for the rest of his life," she explained. "As I grew older, he adored me more. The only time we didn't talk to each other was for eight or nine months when he was shooting *Game of Death*, and that's when he met the girl. I really don't believe there was much of anything sexual between them. If he started to have trouble with me ten years before, I don't think he could be with her that way."

Kim Schmidt, Young's final wife, was born Ruth Hanalore Schmidt in Germany and was raised in Australia. She managed an art gallery and published an art newsletter before becoming a script girl, the job she had when she met Young on the set of the Kung Fu film *Game of Death*. With Bruce Lee dead of a heart attack believed to be related to drug use, the producers salvaged his scenes and wrote a new story. Gig Young said at the time, "What I had to do was act out my part like I was talking to Lee, and then they would splice him in. It certainly was eerie."[70]

By all accounts, Schmidt was very ambitious. She wanted to be famous and live in the United States. Some thought that she saw marrying Young as the ticket to get what she wanted.

Schmidt's mother Rosemary did not believe it was a suicide pact or murder-suicide. In *Final Gig*, Rosemary told author Eells, "I am certain Kim was not killed by her husband but that they were shot by someone else. My husband and I believe someone killed them and so do all their close friends in America."

---

[70] Eells, George. *Final Gig, The Man Behind the Murder*. Orlando, FL: Harcourt, 1st ed., 1991.

The late columnist James Bacon claimed that he had taken calls from people saying that Young was not violent and that he and his wife were murdered because of something in Schmidt's background.

Skye Aubrey says that Schmidt "led a very red tag life. I heard there were drugs and arrests in her past. Gig told me she had Canadian mafia ties. He was very frightened and worried by it. I believe he died because of her.

"Gig was just fed up with the relationship. Even before they got married, it was on again and off again. He was never sure of her, he always questioned her love."

Concerning the Oscar Curse of actors who win Academy Awards ® and then rarely ever get another good role, Aubrey related:

"His career turned to shit after *They Shoot Horses Don't They*. Yes, he was in a downward spiral, but it wasn't that bad. Also, he wasn't an introvert. When he was depressed, he loved to talk. I used to tease him that he bored many an analyst."

Lobby Card - Gig Young in They Shoot Horses Don't They (1969) © Palomar Pictures International, Ltd.— Silver Screen Cinema Collection

Aubrey remembers how she heard the horrible news of her one-time lover and intimate friend's death.

"My father was President of MGM at the time. He heard about Gig's death from a Gold Shield detective…an inside man. My dad came over to my house and told me before it was announced to the media," she remembered with sadness, "Before it was on the air—I knew. The detective told my father that it was a set-up…a hit, but it would never be solved unless someone came forward and confessed. Until then, it will be on the books as a murder-suicide. The whole thing was not up to par. It was very suspicious. The police said that New York is too big. There are too many cases like this."

Aubrey believes that the killers forced their way into the apartment, and many of Young's friends were confused about the guns and ammunition in Young's apartment.

"He had a horror of guns," explains Aubrey. "Anyone who knew Gig would tell you that. One time when we were living together, I had a gun. He made me take it to the police department."

Having lived with Young, Aubrey knew his personal habits. For instance, he was claustrophobic and never dressed in the bathroom.

"They found them both in the bathroom," pointed out Aubrey. "Gig had his tie untied. They were supposed to be going to dinner. Let me tell you, he never got ready in the bathroom and would never be in the same bathroom with a woman. At one time we had a whirlpool tub, and he didn't even want to share that!"

Another important thing Aubrey remembered about Young was his vanity. "Gig used to make me check his nose and ear hairs because he thought that made him look old. He always wanted to be seen at his best. Let's say he wanted to kill himself; he would have set everything up picture perfect and taken pills. It takes some nerve to kill someone and then kill yourself. That wasn't Gig. He was a pacifist. He would never have hurt that girl or himself. I will never ever believe that's what happened."

Young once told interviewer Michael Buckley of *Films in Review,* "You can't tell about people from their outside. They've spent a lifetime covering up their fears."[71]

"Gig was too showbiz to die a bloody death," concluded Skye Aubrey. "He was too vain to die that way. It was not Gig's style. It made no sense at all."

No sense at all…whether a murder-suicide, an accidental shooting followed by suicide or murder…it was just not Gig Young's style.

---

[71] Buckley, Michael. "Gig Young: Were Life Simpler than It Is He'd Have Fared Better," *Films in Review*, February 1971.

CHAPTER 10

Natalie Wood's Final Voyage (1981)

Natalie Wood in the 1970s—Silver Screen Cinema Collection

When Natalie Wood's Russian-born mother Maria was a young girl, she held great faith in superstitions and gypsy, Romany magic. One day she and her sisters had their fortunes read in Harbin, China, where the family had fled following the Russian Bolshevik Revolution. The gypsy cautioned Maria that she should beware of dark water for she was going to drown. The fortuneteller also told Maria that her second daughter would be a great beauty known throughout the world.

Maria always avoided the water, especially dark water, a fear she must have passed down to her daughter through the telling of the tale, because Natalie Wood often said that she liked being near the water, or on the water, but not *in* the water. In an interview just a year before her death, Wood said, "Well, I've always been terrified...still am of water...dark water...sea water...river water. Yet it seems I'm forced to go in the water for every movie I make."[72]

The most important moments of Wood's life with husband Robert Wagner took place on ships. The couple consummated their relationship on Wagner's boat *My Lady*. Wagner wrote in his 2008 autobiography *Pieces of My Heart*, "I remember the instant I fell in love with her. Natalie had the most expressive brown eyes, dark and dancing and deep. One night on the boat, Natalie looked at me with love, her eyes lit by a Coleman lantern that was on top of the table. That was the moment that changed my life." They married twice, the second time in 1972 on the *Ramblin' Rose*, and honeymooned twice in Catalina.

Their final voyage aboard the sixty-foot yacht, the *Splendour*, would also mark the absolute end of their relationship. There would be no divorce and remarriage for the couple this time. No more chances. There would be nothing more for the breathtaking Natalie Wood...her tragic death at the age of forty-three on Thanksgiving weekend of 1981 left her two young daughters motherless and her family, friends, and fans crushed. The event still reverberates to this day.

Wagner has said that some of the best times of his life were on Catalina. It was one of his favorite places in the world, but from the date of Wood's death until now, he has not returned.

---

[72] *Biography*, "Natalie Wood: Child of Hollywood," A & E Television Network, 2003

At the time of this writing, more than three decades after her death, the case has been reopened. The cause of death on her death certificate has changed from "accidental drowning" to "drowning and other undetermined factors." The certificate has now been amended. How she ended up in the cold, dark waters of Catalina are "not clearly established." The Los Angeles Police Department, at the time of this writing, has stated that Robert Wagner is not a suspect.

Natalie Wood

Although she began her career as a child actress, Natalie Wood was never what you could call a "child star." There was no hint of the cutesy mannerisms of some of her contemporaries but instead a sense of seriousness and intelligence beyond her years in her performances. She radiated warmth and grace in every scene. This was particularly evident when she played a war orphan in *Tomorrow is Forever* at the age of eight. Her soft brown eyes reflected every emotion she conveyed on screen. Natalie was one of the few child stars who was able to make a successful transition into adult roles with no awkward period in between. Her explanation of this was: "I just went on working. I was always skinny, and as I got older, I could still play young girls and get by. I was never a child star like Shirley Temple. I always looked like an ordinary kid." Natalie's talent was far from ordinary. Orson Welles once said of his little costar, "She was so good, she frightened me."

Wood was born Natalia Nikolaevna Zakharenko in 1938 to Russian immigrants Nikolai and Maria Zakharenko in San Francisco. Later her father would change the family name to Gurdin because he was tired of being called last for everything. Natalia, nicknamed Natasha by the family, was the middle sister between Olga and Svetlana (Lana). Wood made her film debut at the tender of age of four. Unable to read yet, her sister Olga would read the lines to her, and Natalie would memorize them.

Edmund Gwenn and Natalie Wood in Miracle on 34th Street
© 20th Century Fox—Silver Screen Cinema Collection

Perhaps her most memorable childhood role was that of Susan, the little girl too sensible to believe in Santa Claus in *Miracle on 34th Street* (1947). This holiday film favorite did, in fact, run on television in Los Angeles on the day of her untimely death.

Maureen O'Hara, who played her mother in the film, recalled her screen daughter on *E! True Hollywood Story*, "She knew what she was supposed to do before anyone told her. She was that good."

O'Hara also recalls having had great fun with Wood when they filmed *Miracle on 34th Street* at Macy's at night when the department store was closed. "Natalie and I had a wonderful time because we'd sneak off, and with nobody in the store, we were able to go through every department and try on all sorts of things that we had no right to do whatsoever. But we really enjoyed it. It was wonderful."

Even though Wood played a skeptical child, O'Hara says, "Natalie was convinced that Edmund Gwenn was Santa Claus. He was jolly and kind and wonderful."[73]

Wood's fear of water actually became a full-fledged phobia when she made *The Green Promise* (1949). In this film she had to run across a specially rigged bridge that was set to collapse after Wood crossed over it. The bridge collapsed too soon, and the director insisted on letting the cameras roll on the terrified child. The shot stayed in the film.

Wood fractured her wrist and almost drowned. Wood's mother refused to take her to a doctor. She didn't want her daughter to seem to be too much trouble or a high maintenance child star. As a result of the injury from this accident, Wood had a distended wrist bone. She wore a wide bracelet (which she nicknamed the Badge) to hide what she considered a deformity for the rest of her life.

Stage Mother Maria Gurdin also manipulated her daughter in order to make sure she cried on cue, by pulling the wings off a butterfly and forcing young Natalie to re-live her beloved dog being run over and killed.

In an interview, Wood once reflected on her years as a child actress. "I got a lot of good training because I often played the daughter of very famous actors. So I got a chance to work with them and have sort of on-the-spot training, as it were…instead of going off to acting school.

"I had worked so much, you know, since I was a child all during my childhood that really by the time I was twenty or twenty-one, I didn't have a very clear perception of myself. I was always Bette Davis's daughter or Maureen O'Hara's daughter or Jimmy Stewart's daughter or something like that. I was sort of discombobulated."[74]

It seems in many of her films, including *Splendor in the Grass* (1961) and *The Star* (1952), Natalie was required to film scenes in the water. The gypsy premonition story from her mother combined with the accident she suffered from *The Green Promise* made Wood even more terrified of film-

---

[73] *E! True Hollywood Story*, "Natalie Wood," "E" Entertainment Television Network, December 14, 1997

[74] *Biography*, "Natalie Wood: Child of Hollywood," A & E Television Network, 2003

ing in the water. Her screen mother in *The Star*, Bette Davis, came to her defense when director Stuart Heisler insisted Wood jump into the ocean and swim to a raft. He would not listen to the child's protests. At the 1977 American Film Institute Bette Davis tribute, Wood recalled Davis's threat to leave the film unless a stunt double was used. "This was the only time I saw the famous Bette Davis temperament surface —and it was not on her own behalf."

At eleven years old, Wood was playing eight-year olds and was extremely annoyed about portraying characters younger than herself. By the time she was fourteen, Wood was already developing into a lovely young starlet. She barely had an awkward stage.

*Natalie Wood on the set of Rebel Without a Cause
(1955)/Warner Bros. with James Dean and director
Nicholas Ray—Historical Editorial Archive*

The turning point in Wood's career from child to more mature roles came in 1955 when she co-starred with James Dean and Sal Mineo in *Rebel without a Cause* (1955). Her mother didn't want her to be in a film about rebellious teens. Wood later remembered that she had threatened to run away and become a real juvenile delinquent if her parents wouldn't let her play the part. Nicholas Ray, the director of *Rebel without a Cause*, was also not confident that she could handle the role and was testing other actresses.

One night Wood was out with Dennis Hopper who did have a role in *Rebel without a Cause*. Hopper was driving on Laurel Canyon; it had been raining and was slippery. Hopper skidded into a head-on collision with another car. Hopper, Wood, and another passenger were thrown from the vehicle. Wood later remembered that she demanded that Nicholas Ray be notified, not her parents. When she saw Ray, she pulled him to her and whispered, "Nick! They called me a goddamn juvenile delinquent. Now do I get the part?"[75]

Wood, who grew to be an exquisite, exotic beauty, received the first of three Academy Award ® nominations. The first was for her portrayal of the misunderstood teenager in *Rebel without a Cause*. The other two were for *Splendor in the Grass* (1961) and *Love with the Proper Stranger* (1963). Wood once described the effect working with James Dean in *Rebel without a Cause* had on her career, "It was the first time I had any feelings about a role. James taught me to relax before playing tense. I had never thought of acting that way before."

The sixteen-year-old actress also entered into romances with Dennis Hopper and forty-two-year-old director Nicholas Ray. She also dated Scott Marlowe and, very briefly, Elvis Presley.

The Sixties were perhaps Wood's most productive decade creatively. She gave stellar performances in her films that reflected the time period they were made in. *West Side Story* (1961) dealt with racial prejudice; *Inside Daisy Clover* (1966) exposed the harsh side of stardom behind the glamour, and the satire *Bob & Carol & Ted & Alice* (1969), where Wood played a middle class housewife, looked at embracing free love and the new morality. This film was to be the last hugely successful theatrical film Wood would make. Wood wisely waived her salary for a percentage of the profits *for Bob & Carol & Ted & Alice*, which resulted in a huge financial windfall for her.

---

75   Finstad, Suzanne. *Natasha: The Biography of Natalie Wood*. New York, NY: Harmony Books, 2001.

Lobby Card - Bob & Carol & Ted & Alice -
Dyan Cannon and Natalie Wood, © Columbia
Pictures—Silver Screen Cinema Collection

During the 1970s and 1980, Wood would give some exceptional performances in television films such as *Cat on a Hot Tin Roof* with Robert Wagner and Sir Laurence Olivier (whom she greatly admired), and in *The Cracker Factory* and the miniseries *From Here to Eternity*, both from 1979. Wood was at her best playing emotionally fragile characters, as she did so expertly in *Splendor in the Grass* and *The Cracker Factory.*

Robert Wagner

Robert John Wagner Jr. was born in Detroit, in 1930, the son of a wealthy steel tycoon. He attended military academies as a child and was expected to follow in the family business. Following the family's move to California, one of the teenage Wagner's jobs was as a caddy at the Bel-Air Country Club. Wagner carried golf clubs for stars like Clark Gable, Randolph Scott, Bing Crosby, Cary Grant, and Alan Ladd. An enthusiastic star-struck kid, he continuously asked them questions about the movie business and drank in all their answers. By the time he was in his early twenties, Darryl Zanuck had Wagner signed up with a 20th Century Fox contract.

Wagner was given the complete star build-up. Learning the value of publicity early, he was good-natured and cooperative with the press. His first memorable role was in *With a Song in My Heart* (1952) with Susan Hayward, who portrayed singer Jane Froman. Wagner played a shell-shocked soldier that Hayward sang to. Another important film role for the young Wagner was *Titanic* (1953). It was during that film that the twenty-two-year-old Wagner and forty-five-year-old Barbara Stanwyck began a love affair that lasted four years. In that era, an older woman and younger man couldn't date openly in Hollywood. It would have been quite a scandal. Today, Stanwyck would be celebrated as a cougar.

The Mountain (1956) and *Broken Lance* (1954) were two films Wagner did with Spencer Tracy, who became a surrogate father to him. At a 2008 book signing in Palm Springs, Wagner spoke of Tracy. "Spencer Tracy was like a father to me. He changed my career. I did a film called *The Mountain*, and he gave me co-star billing above the title, which was a very big thing for him to do. It took me out of being just another good-looking guy in Hollywood.

"I made the mistake one day of trying to underplay Tracy. He said, 'I couldn't hear that line.' I said, 'Boy, that's something, if I'm underplaying you.' At lunchtime, he took me into his trailer, and he really let me have it. He said, 'You shouldn't be thinking about things like that; you should be thinking about how you're going to play the part. Don't learn the tricks of the trade, learn the trade.' As a matter of fact, I thought he was going to take me out of the film. He didn't…thank God."

In the sixties, Wagner was in hits such as *The Pink Panther* (1963) with Peter Sellers and his good friend David Niven, and *Harper* (1966) with Paul Newman. He enjoyed his biggest success in television from the sixties to the eighties in *It Takes a Thief* (where Fred Astaire had a recurring role as Wagner's character's father); *Switch* with Eddie Albert; and *Hart to Hart* with Stephanie Powers. When it was suggested that Natalie Wood co-star in *Hart to Hart*, Wagner said, "I sell soap. My wife sells tickets."

In recent years he's had great success with guest spots on *Two and a Half Men* and *NCIS* on television and as Number 2 in the Austin Powers franchise.

Robert Wagner and Natalie Wood

Ten-year-old Natalie Wood first laid eyes on eighteen-year-old Robert Wagner, wearing army fatigues for a film, as he walked down the corridor at 20th Century Fox. She turned to her mother and said, "I'm going to marry him," and she did just that…twice. Wagner has said, "I had to take Natalie's word, because I don't remember any of it. She always told me we didn't speak but that I smiled."[76]

After dating for one year, Wagner took Wood to Romanoff's where he poured champagne. He had placed a diamond and pearl engagement ring at the bottom of the glass. They married just weeks later, on December 28, 1957.

For the first few years, their marriage was good. While on suspension from Warner Brothers, Wood began seeing a psychoanalyst every day. Her mother had instilled a lot of fears in her, and her childhood was lost to working. While Wood's career began to soar with films such as *West Side Story* and *Splendor in The Grass*, Wagner's career was stalled.

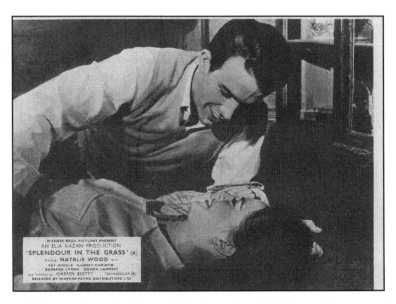

Lobby Card - Splendor in The Grass (1961) Warren Beatty and Natalie Wood © Warner Bros.—Silver Screen Cinema Collection

---

[76] Wagner, Robert. *Pieces of My Heart*. New York: IT Books Reprint Edition, 2009

Director Elia Kazan said there was an affair between Wood and her co-star Warren Beatty during the filming of *Splendor in the Grass*. Wagner says he believes the affair didn't begin until after the break-up with his wife. Wagner did admit to feeling jealous of Wood because "she attracted every man around her." He also felt that Wood going to analysis was somehow a failure on his part. After a huge argument in June of 1961, they separated. Wagner read and heard of Beatty and Wood's affair and was incensed.

"I wanted to kill the son-of-a-bitch," Wagner wrote in his autobiography. "The one thing I did not want to have happen was have him move into my life and break up my marriage. That was the absolute bottom. I felt as if the ground was being systematically cut from beneath me. I was also totally humiliated in a way I'd never felt before and, thank god, have never felt since."[77]

Wagner admitted to waiting outside Beatty's house with a gun, hoping he'd walk out. He said he was on the verge of an emotional breakdown. He thought if he couldn't kill Beatty, he'd kill himself. A good friend, John Foreman, helped Wagner, and ironically he went into analysis, which was a point of argument with Wood during their marriage.

Wagner left for Europe to make films, and Wood filed for divorce. After Wood's affair with Beatty ended, it's reported that she set fire to his clothes. Following Beatty, Wood had romances with a string of men, including a brief engagement to Arthur Loew Jr. and a romance with Michael Caine and former co-star Steve McQueen.

Wagner met Marion Marshall Donen, ex-wife of director Stanley Donen in Europe. They married and had a daughter, Katie, in 1964. Strangely enough, when Wagner was at La Scala restaurant handing out cigars and sharing the happy news, he ran into Wood. The thought of Wagner having a child with another woman depressed her. She told her sister Lana that she just had to have a baby.

Wood began to date British agent/director Richard Gregson and married him in 1969. Her daughter Natasha, the mirror image of her exquisitely beautiful mother, was born in 1970. Wood discovered Gregson was having an affair with their secretary and immediately threw him out. The locks were changed; Gregson couldn't even drive up to the house. When

---

[77] Wagner, Robert. *Pieces of My Heart*. New York: IT Books Reprint Edition, 2009

Robert Wagner and Natalie Wood in London (AP Photo 1972)

she decided the marriage was finished, it was completely finished.

Wood and Wagner had run into each other from time to time over the years, including when Natalie was expecting Natasha, and realized that they still had feelings for one another. Wagner was briefly engaged to Tina Sinatra. Once free of their respective romantic entanglements, the couple finally got together again, re-marrying on a friend's yacht, the *Ramblin' Rose*, in 1972.

"When RJ and I met ten years later, after our divorce, we were different people. It wasn't like going back to what we had before because we had both changed," recalled Wood. "We were still attracted to one another—there's always something about your first love. It was like getting to know a whole new person, although somewhere in the back of your mind—you already knew them."

Wood happily semi-retired for a time to devote her energies to her family, which had a new addition, Courtney Brook Wagner, born in 1974. Concerning her screen hiatus and motherhood, Wood once said, "I love acting, and I know I could have been working all the time. There was a period in my life where I just went from picture to picture. I really didn't have any other life. I felt rather empty, and I guess I was. You must be able to give something back in life. I've discovered being a mother puts things into wonderful perspective. I'm so happy I'm terrified! You can be working on a set where everything seems a matter of life and death, when suddenly you get a phone call that one of your kids has come down with a fever. All at once, that becomes much more important than some movie where an actor is throwing a tantrum on the set."[78]

The Splendor—Thanksgiving Weekend 1981

After her children grew a little older, Wood became restless. The artist in her wanted to work and be creative again. Wagner preferred that she be home with the children. When she costarred with William Devane, filming a nude love scene, in *From Here to Eternity*, Wagner wrote that a warning bell went off in his head because of his experience with Warren Beatty and *Splendor in the Grass*. His concern turned out to be unfounded.

Wagner said the bell went off again when Wood was shooting a science fiction film, *Brainstorm*, on location in North Carolina with Christopher Walken, one of the hottest young actors in the business at the time.

On Thanksgiving Day, Wood's nine-year-old daughter Natasha became completely hysterical at the thought of her mother leaving for a Catalina Island weekend vacation. She begged her mother to stay home. In addition to Wagner and Wood, others were invited on the trip; however, only one guest would be able to go along, Wood's co-star Walken. It was not unusual for the couple to take their fellow actors and costars on trips.

It was a rough crossing on Friday afternoon. Walken began the voyage with Bloody Marys, became seasick, and spent the afternoon sleeping, waking once the yacht was moored in Avalon, Catalina.

The Captain, Dennis Davern, stayed on the *Splendour* to prepare their dinner, while Wagner, Wood, and Walken went to El Galleon for margaritas. It was a stormy night, and the trio returned to the ship for dinner around nine o'clock in the evening. Walken felt seasick again and went to his cabin. He overheard an argument. Wood was angry at Wagner for being suspicious of her relationship with Walken and for insisting on moving the boat to the Isthmus on the other side of the island. According to Davern, Wagner didn't want to be seen in public in Avalon with Wood and Walken, feeling like a third wheel, and preferred the more rustic, private side of the island. Wood insisted that Davern take her back to Avalon on the dinghy,

---

[78]   Kulzer, Dina-Marie, Natalie Wood: A Tribute http://www.classichollywoodbios. com/nataliewood.htm

the Valiant. They booked two rooms at the Pavilion Lodge; however, Wood did not want to be alone. So they shared the same room and bed but were not intimate, according to Davern. Wood hated to be alone and was still riddled with the fears and insecurities imposed on her by her mother. She often wanted someone in the room with her.

Wood talked about leaving the island, which Davern thought was a good idea. She made calls to her friend Mart Crowley and her stepson Josh Donen. She wanted someone to meet the helicopter in case she decided to return to the mainland. She left a third message for Donen saying that everything was fine, and she would stay on the island.

The next morning, tempers seemed to have cooled. Wood came back to the boat and made *huevos rancheros* for everyone. This time, when Wagner suggested moving the *Splendour* to Isthmus Cove, Wood agreed.

The whole party took an afternoon nap following their previous night of drinking. Walken and Wood awoke first and took the dinghy to Doug's Harbor Reef, the only restaurant/bar on that side of the island. They left a note for Wagner who joined them later. They drank until seven o'clock in the evening and then went to have dinner where the drinking continued. At one point, Wood threw her wine glass, smashing it, according to witnesses. They left at ten o'clock to return to the *Splendour*, and the restaurant manager notified the Harbor Patrol that the party had too much to drink.

The drinking continued aboard the *Splendour*. There was an argument. Wagner said at first it was a political discourse and later said the argument was over Walken encouraging Wood to put her career first. According to Wagner, he said, "Why the fuck don't you stay out of her career?" According to Davern, Wagner actually said, "So what do you want to do, fuck my wife? Is that what you want?"[79] Wagner smashed a wine bottle. When the police initially asked about the smashed bottle, they were told it was because of rough seas. Decades later, Wagner admitted smashing the bottle during the argument.

---

[79] Rulli, Marti, and Dennis Davern. *Goodbye Natalie, Goodbye Splendour*. New York: E-Rights/E-Reads Ltd. Publishers, 2009

Davern says he picked up on Wagner's jealousy and animosity during the trip, and that Wagner felt the odd man out while his wife flirted with the younger actor.

Wagner told CBS news, "I looked below, and I saw Natalie was doing something with her hair. She was going to go to bed. She shut the door. Chris and I were still talking. When I went down below, she wasn't there. The dinghy was gone. I looked around, and I didn't know where she was."

"She slipped on the swim step at the stern and was either stunned or knocked unconscious and rolled into the water. The loose dinghy floated away. We were so in love, and we had everything. And in a second it was gone. I wasn't there. I wasn't there for her, and that's always within me."[80]

Christopher Walken, when not in town on Catalina, seemed to have been sleeping or seasick most of the trip, told Lawrence Grobel of *Playboy* magazine in 1997, "Anybody there saw the logistics—of the boat, the night, where we were, that it was raining—and would know exactly what happened. You hear about things happening to people, they slip in the bathtub, fall down the stairs, step off a curb in London because they think that the cars come the other way, and they die. You feel you want to die making an effort at something; you don't want to die in some unnecessary way.

"What happened that night only she knows, because she was alone. She had gone to bed before us, and her room was at the back. A dinghy was bouncing against the boat, and I think she went out to move it. There was a ski ramp that was partially in the water, it was slippery—I had walked on it myself. She had told me she couldn't swim. In fact, they had to cut a swimming scene from *Brainstorm*. She was probably half asleep, and she was wearing a coat."[81]

Olga Virapeff, Wood's older sister, has said, "The guys were all up there getting loaded...who knows what happened?"[82]

---

[80] *48 Hours*, "Vanity Fair: Hollywood Scandal," November 19, 2011

[81] Grobel, Lawrence. Christopher Walken Interview, *Playboy Magazine*. Sage Publications, Inc. September 1997.

[82] Finstad, Suzanne. *Natasha: The Biography of Natalie Wood*. New York, NY: Harmony Books, 2001.

Davern has been giving out information piecemeal for decades. First his story agreed with Wagner's. He claims he remained quiet at Wagner's behest. In interviews and his book *Goodbye Natalie, Goodbye Splendour*, co-authored with Marti Rulli, he states that he was kept close to the family after the tragedy…and goes as far to say that he was actually monitored. Davern said he was a close friend to Wagner, and every effort was made to keep their stories straight. He felt he was a real friend to the family, certainly while Wood was alive, and he comforted Wagner and was a drinking companion, once she was gone.

Davern resided at the Wagner home for a time and then went back to the *Splendour* to live and to prepare it for sale. Unable to sell the yacht, Wagner donated it to the Sea Scouts. Davern was angry about not getting his commission, since the yacht was donated instead of sold.

For a while, Wagner helped Davern work as a film extra. Once the *Splendour* was gone, the friendship between Davern and Wagner was over. The film extra work and salary ceased. Davern said he'd get a thousand here and there from Wagner for working on the *Splendour* before it was donated. Whether it was the termination of the money or friendship, Davern began to tell a different story about the night Wood drowned. It seems he was more hurt by the end of the friendship than the end of the job.

Davern's first story was that at approximately eleven o'clock, Wagner noticed Wood was not in her stateroom. He told Davern to look around the ship. Davern asked to put the searchlights on, and Wagner said no. He then asked to radio for help, and again his request was refused.

John Payne and his fiancée Marilyn Wayne were on a nearby boat—the *Capricorn* In an interview with author Suzanne Finstad, they said that at 11:05 p.m., they heard a woman screaming, "Somebody please help me. I'm drowning." They heard a man answer, "Oh, don't worry, we'll help you. Hold your hat; we're coming to get you."[83] When the cries for help continued, they called the harbormaster. There was no answer. They called Avalon and were told a helicopter was coming. The helicopter never came.

---

[83] Finstad, Suzanne. *Natasha: The Biography of Natalie Wood.* New York, NY: Harmony Books, 2001.

The *Capicorn's* dinghy was deflated to they couldn't search themselves. At 11:25 p.m. the cries for help stopped.

At one thirty Wagner called the manager of Doug's Harbor Reef to look for Wood. He didn't want to call the coast guard in a desire to keep it low key. He didn't want the bad publicity if his wife had taken the dinghy and gone to the bar/restaurant. At two thirty they called the harbormaster. The coast guard wasn't called until three thirty. Reportedly, Wagner's attorney was telephoned from the *Splendour* before the coast guard, who was called four hours after Wood was noticed to be missing.

The dinghy was discovered at five thirty with the oars in disarray and the ignition in the off position. At a quarter to eight, Wood was found floating in the water upright. She was wearing a flannel nightgown, socks, no underwear, and a red down jacket that acted as a life preserver. The jacket kept her floating. Coroner Thomas Noguchi originally said the jacket would weigh her down; in fact it did just the opposite. Wood's autopsy report states that she had two dozen bruises. A new autopsy report supplement released to the public in January of 2013 notes, "bruises, especially in the upper extremities, appeared fresh and could have occurred before (Wood) entered the water." It also notes that, "the location of the bruises, the multiplicity of the bruises, lack of head trauma, or facial bruising support bruising having occurred prior to entry in the water."[84]

Restaurant owner Doug Bombard and lifeguard Roger Smith pulled Wood out of the water. Smith said she was beautiful even in death. Her brown eyes were open, and he closed them. "All I remember is her eyes." Davern was asked by Wagner to identify the body as he couldn't face it himself.

In the decades following Wood's tragic death, Davern has been interviewed for the tabloids and has been on various television programs. He had been in contact with his friend, author Marti Rulli. Little by little he provided tortured recollections of that night. Yet the stories have been

---

[84] Goffard, Christopher, Kate Mather and Richard Winton, "New Twist in Wood's Death", *Los Angeles Times*, January 15, 2013

inconsistent over the decades. At a1992 taping of Geraldo Rivera's *Now It Can Be Told*, Rulli was reported to have said, not realizing she was on a hidden camera, that they could make billions off the book if Davern could say how Wood got in the water. She later said her comments were misinterpreted.

Davern remembered a huge argument between the couple in the stateroom, with things being slammed around and thumping noises. Wagner told Davern to leave when he knocked on the door. He then recalled that the argument continued on deck, and then Wagner put the red down jacket on Wood. They were arguing; one minute she was there and the next she was not.

These latent memories came after Davern was hypnotized in 2008, twenty-seven years following Wood's death. He then took a polygraph test that he passed.

Lana Wood, younger sister of Natalie Wood, remembered that a day or so after Wood's death, Wagner was terribly distraught. "My recollection is that he said something like, "It was in an accident. It was something that wasn't meant to be."

Lana also recalled phone calls she received from Davern to TMZ.

"Dennis called me late one night. He did seem like he had been drinking. He was crying, and he said that he never meant to hurt anybody. He didn't tell the truth because he felt he would be held responsible in some way. That frightened him for a long time. He wasn't incredibly specific. He said everybody was quite drunk. He said a fight, I should say an argument, broke out, and that Natalie was in the water, and that he and RJ did nothing to pull her out. He said—this is a direct quote from what Dennis said to me, 'Leave her there and teach her a lesson.' I told him to go to the authorities. He said, 'I'll be implicated.'"

When asked what she thought happened to her sister, Lana said, "Nobody knows what happened except RJ. That's the only person who really knows. I believe that she was in the water and that she was panicky. And I think she drowned before anybody could do anything. I can't ever believe that RJ would purposefully do anything to hurt her. I honestly, from my heart, believe that it was drink, and people being out of control and not thinking clearly…and just high emotions. In that case it would be an accident. I would just be happy, personally, if the truth was out there. The truth is so easy to do. I just want to know once and for all. Natalie was a wonderful person. And I think she deserves the truth and deserves to rest."[85]

85   Lana Wood, Captain Says Wagner Left Wood To Teach Her a Lesson; http://www.tmz.com/2011/11/18/natalie-wood-sister-lana-wood-robert-wagner-video-homicide-investigation/

CHAPTER 11

Robert Blake–In Cold Blood (2001)

Robert Blake—Silver Screen Cinema Collection

Breaking the calm of a quiet, slightly breezy, Friday evening, May 4, 2001, filmmaker Sean Stanek was startled by his doorbell ringing incessantly and a fierce, continuous pounding on his door. He opens the door to find sixty-seven-year-old actor Robert Blake, clothed totally in black and wearing a black cap, standing on his porch. A shaking, crying, vomiting Blake is screaming, "She's hurt! I need help! Dear God, please someone help me!"

Blake had Stanek call 911 and then took him to his 1991 black Dodge Stealth that was parked across the street. The car was parked under a burned-out streetlight and behind a construction Dumpster. There, Stanek found Blake's wife of six months, Bonny Lee Bakley, slumped in the front seat of the car, hardly breathing and bleeding profusely. Blake rushed back to Vitello's restaurant in Studio City, California, where he and Bakley had dined earlier, to find a doctor.

Stanek, left alone with Bakley and on the phone with a 911 operator, tried to halt the bleeding from her head by soaking up the blood with a towel. She was barely breathing and had two bullet wounds in her right cheek and right shoulder. Stanek asked her if she could hear his voice to squeeze his hand. Bakley did not respond except to make gurgling noises. He noted that the interior of the car was splattered with blood, that the window on the passenger side was rolled down, and that there was no shattered glass.

This wasn't the first time Blake left Bakley alone during their evening out. After they finished dinner, the couple walked a block and a half to their car on Woodbridge Street where the actor chose to park rather than leaving the car with the valet in the restaurant parking lot, as was his usual custom. Blake claimed that he suddenly remembered he had left his gun, a Smith and Wesson 38 Special (for which he had a concealed weapon permit), at the restaurant and had his wife remain in the car while he went back to retrieve it.

Patrons of Vitello's and co-owner Joseph Restivo recalled that a distraught, panic-stricken Blake came back to the restaurant just once following the shooting, and no one remembered seeing him look for a gun. The only time anyone remembered seeing him was when he came back to try and get medical help for his wife.

The table was bussed minutes after the couple's departure. No gun was found. Restivo claimed Blake had alternately said his wife had been hurt, had fallen, and then finally admitted that she had been shot. Blake drank two glasses of water while at the restaurant. Stanek gave him several more glasses of water when he returned to Woodbridge Street. Blake had been vomiting since finding Bakley. He later said when he first saw her that he originally thought she had fainted or had some kind of seizure. His vomiting was originally attributed to the shock of finding his wife. Friends, however, have said this was Blake's custom: to eat a huge dinner, drink a lot of club soda, and then vomit. It was how he kept his weight down. A restaurant patron claimed that earlier in the evening Blake was pulling at his hair, murmuring to himself, and vomiting in the men's room of Vitello's.

As the paramedics arrived, Blake asked Stanek. "What's going on, is she dead, is she dead?"

Blake handed over his Smith and Wesson, which no one saw at the restaurant, to the police. It was later determined not to be the murder weapon. The murder weapon, a rare German World War II-era Walther PPK pistol, was later found in a nearby trash bin. The pistol was freshly oiled so there were no fingerprints. The serial number on the pistol had been partially filed off as is customary in professional contract killings.

Bonnie Lee Bakley, just a month short of her forty-fifth birthday, was pronounced dead on arrival at St. Joseph's Medical Center in Burbank, California. Blake refused the police request to take a polygraph test because he said he had had "dreams" of killing her and felt that might affect the results. The night of his wife's murder, an agitated Blake spent the night in the hospital due to high blood pressure.

Crime reconstructionist and former homicide detective Rod Englert was hired by prosecutor Shellie Samuels to examine the evidence. In his book *Blood Secrets* Englert revealed that Luminol tests revealed no traces of blood splatter on Blake's clothing.

"We traced the trajectory of each bullet wound based on Bakley's injuries," wrote Englert. "We started by working backward from the termination point of the bullet lodged in the left side of her head to its entry point in her body—a hole low on the right side of her jaw. Then we did the same with the shoulder wound. Both bullets remained lodged in Bakley's body, and both would have been fatal. To understand the path the bullets took, we envisioned an imaginary steel rod running from each termination point back through each entry point. If Bakley had been seated in a normal upright position, the rods would have run downward through the car door to a point of origin in the pavement.

"But there were no bullet holes in the Stealth's door. Whoever shot Bakley fired through the open car window. That meant she saw her killer pointing a gun at her and leaned to the left toward the driver's side in a classic defensive posture. She didn't have time to do anything else to protect herself. In my opinion, the first bullet struck her in the head and the second hit her shoulder, though I couldn't be certain. Expirated blood covering the gearshift showed that she slumped farther to her left after she was hit and exhaled blood onto it in her last moments of life."[86]

Gunpowder residue tests on Blake's hands were later found to be inconclusive. Blake's first attorney Harland Braun told the press that the tests were negative. There was no gunpowder on his hands and no bloody blowback on his clothing. Robert Blake did not fire the pistol that killed his wife.

Bonny Lee Bakley

Bonny Lee Bakley was born in 1956 in Morristown, New Jersey. Her father Edward, a tree surgeon, and her mother Marjorie were constantly at each other's throats. The family was dirt poor, and their home life was extremely volatile. Reportedly, when Bakley was a little girl, she used to pass out whenever they fought. In 1963 her parents broke up, and Bonny, her sister Margerry, and brother Joey never saw their father again. Edward Bakley died in the drunk tank of the Morristown jail ten years later. Bakely's younger sister Margerry revealed to Dennis McDougal and Mary Murphy, authors of *Blood Cold*, of her father, "The drunken bum molested my sister."[87]

---

[86]   Englert, Rod, and Kathy Passero. *Blood Secrets: Chronicles of a Crime Scene Reconstructionist.* New York: Thomas Dunne Books, 2010.

[87]   McDougal, Dennis and Mary Murphy. *Blood Cold: Fame Sex and Murder in Hollywood*, New York: Onyx, 2002.

Bakley ended up moving in with her grandmother Margaret Hall while still a toddler. Bonny's mother borrowed money from Hall who insisted that Bonny be given to her as collateral for the loan. Following Edward Bakley's death and due to the fact that the loan was never paid back, her grandmother kept Bonny and raised her as her own.

Grandmother Hall took thriftiness to an extreme and didn't believe in wasting water, so Bonny was not allowed to bathe or wash her hair very often. This, along with the hand-me-down clothes she wore, made her the cruel butt of jokes at school. The things that made her happy were Elvis records and *American*

Bonny Lee Bakley,
Historical Editorial Archive

Bandstand. Like many little girls, she dreamed of becoming famous. When a friend later asked why she was so attracted to men in show business, she said it was because she wanted to be famous herself. "You think," said Bakley, "I'll show them (the children who ridiculed her)—I'll become a movie star."

As Bakley grew into an appealing, pretty young woman, she came to realize that she could use her sexuality to get what she wanted. As a young girl, she frequented a nudist colony near the trailer park where she lived with her grandmother. From there, she began entering nudist beauty pageants, and at the age of seventeen, she began offering herself as a model for nude pictures in classified ads. This was the start of what would later become a mail order and phone sex business that would become successful enough for her to hire her family members. In fact, at the time of her death, Bakley left an estate of $500,000.00, including property in Southern California. She was obviously good at what she did.

Bakley graduated from nude modeling to becoming a grifter and con artist who bilked men out of money. She'd ask for cash for bus fare, car repairs, and airline tickets and promise to visit these men and fulfill their sexual fantasies. In most cases, she never visited them at all.

Bakley's first husband was a Greek immigrant, Evangelos Paulikis, who married her because he wanted a green card. Her sister Margerry said, "The asshole beat her so she had him deported."

Her sex schemes grew from asking impressionable men for money to marrying them and getting them to deed property over to her or make her a beneficiary on their life insurance policies. Investigations by police and private detectives hired by Robert Blake after Bakley's murder revealed she may have married as many as ten times…the legality of these marriages is questionable.

Her illicit activities included drug charges, misrepresentation of the value of property, and passing bad checks, including one for $600,000.00. She was later caught in Arkansas with seven driver's licenses and five social security cards. She used these IDs to rent post office boxes under different names for her mail order sex/lonely hearts schemes.

Bakley's obsession with celebrity really took hold when she went to a Frankie Valli and the Four Seasons concert when she was twelve years old. It was the highlight of her young life. Her husband and cousin Paul Gawron, the father of three of her children, once said, "She decided right then and there that she was going to get him." For twenty years she followed Valli around the country, staying in the same hotels he did and waiting outside his dressing room to no avail.

After working as a film extra and model in New York and California under the name Leebonny, she discovered that becoming a movie star was a daunting task. She would set her sights, ambition, and all her ingenuity on marrying a famous star. Her targets included Dean Martin, Gary Busey, and most notably, Jerry Lee Lewis, Christian Brando, and, of course, Robert Blake. The money she made from her mail order sex business would fund these trips to California to chase potential famous husbands.

During the 1990s, Bakley stalked singer Jerry Lee Lewis. Using the same method of operation as she had with Frankie Valli, she followed him and took it a step further by befriending Lewis's sisters. Linda Gail Lewis told *Murder in Hollywood* author Gary C. King, "She was a groupie and she really wanted to meet my brother and she did." While pursuing Lewis, Bakley was also seeing Marlon Brando's son Christian, who had been convicted of killing his sister Cheyenne's lover Dag Drollet in 1991. "She was spending every weekend in a penal farm and seeing Christian Brando," explained Lewis. "She didn't tell me how she hooked up with him, but I was amazed by it." Bakley's sister Margerry said, "It was her life's dream to marry a movie star and have a baby."[88]

In July 1993 Bakley gave birth to a daughter she named Jeri Lee Lewis and claimed that the entertainer was the child's father. Jerry Lee Lewis denied parentage, saying he was out of the country at the time the child was conceived, and he had passport records to prove it. "I don't know if the DNA tests proved the little girl was his baby," said Lewis's sister Linda. "But I think there was some settlement."

A week following Bakley's death, Jerry Lee Lewis released a statement to the press that said, in part, "I do hope the child who has my name and has been told I am her father learns that I am not her father and that I am very sorry she has had to suffer this lie. I have always taken care of my children and have never denied any of my children. I have lost two sons already. The lives of my children are very dear and precious to me."

Bakley left her infant daughter with her former husband Paul Gawron. She sent money to him for the care and support of all three of her children. Gawron later told reporters, "I don't know for sure if any of these kids are biologically mine."[89] He described how Bakley would have her porn materials spread all over the room with the children running in and out. Gawron didn't like it but had little to say about it. It was more lucrative to work with Bakley than as a low-paid laborer.

---

[88]   King, Gary C.. *Murder In Hollywood: The Secret Life and Mysterious Death of Bonny Lee Bakley*. New York: St. Martin's Paperbacks, 2001.

[89]   McDougal, Dennis and Mary Murphy. *Blood Cold: Fame Sex and Murder in Hollywood*, New York: Onyx, 2002.

At the time of Bakely's death, the press contacted Gawron. "A reporter called and told me that she had been killed. I wasn't surprised. She always was a dreamer. She chased her dream, and it killed her."

Robert Blake

Robert Blake was born Michael James Vincenzo Gubitosi in 1933 in Nutley, New Jersey. His parents James and Elizabeth had a song and dance act that eventually included their children…they were billed as The Little Hillbillies. The family moved to Los Angeles in 1936 where they found work as movie extras.

"I'm lonely. I was born lonely, and I'll die lonely," Blake explained in a 2012 CNN interview with Piers Morgan. "God kept me alive in the womb when my mother tried to abort me twice with coat hangers." Blake has said that his real father was not James Gubitosi but his brother Tony. "I was a pain in the ass to them. They had two kids, two abortions. And then she got pregnant again, but she really got pregnant with my uncle across the street, because that's who she's really in love with. Now she's pregnant with me. My uncle tells her to go to hell and runs off. She hates me. My father hates me because in his heart he knows I'm his brother's kid. They tried to get rid of me. And they couldn't. They didn't have the fifteen dollars to pay Frank Sinatra's mother, alleged to have been an abortionist in New Jersey, for the abortion."[90]

In many interviews over the years before and after the murder, Blake has talked about the abuse he suffered at the hands of his father, which was ignored by his cold, complacent mother. He claims he was locked up in closets at the age of one or two, burned, treated like a dog, and sexually molested. He was smoking cigarettes at the age of five.

Once in Los Angeles, Blake graduated from being a two dollars a day extra in *The Little Rascals/Our Gang* series to becoming a regular in 1938. Even as a small child, he was looking for a break. Another child actor had trouble saying the line, "Confidentially, it stinks." So Blake said the line and that eventually led to the role of Mickey.

---

[90] *Piers Morgan Tonight*, "Robert Blake," Cable News Network, July 11, 2012

Blake became the family breadwinner, and his family was envious of his success. Years later his mother, older brother, and sister would deny the abuse ever occurred. His father James committed suicide at age forty-eight. His niece Noreen Austin, the only family member Blake remained close to, said the abuse absolutely did happen.

Young Robert Blake and Donna Reed in Mokey (1942)
© MGM—Silver Screen Cinema Collection

In Blake's outstanding 2011 book *Tales of a Rascal – What I did for Love,* he relates memories of Elizabeth Taylor reading Edgar Allen Poe to him on the MGM schoolhouse porch, and the day he got the title role of *Mokey* (1942), a film with Donna Reed who gave him more affection than his own mother. It was at this time that the head of MGM, Louis B. Mayer, told him that his name Mickey Gubitosi would no longer do as his name. He was christened Bobby Blake and told "Now you're one of us." His ethnicity was erased with the change of his name. This meant that Blake could no longer have lunch with his *Little Rascals* co-star Buckwheat. Blacks were not allowed to sit in the commissary, so the boys continued eating together at the lunch counter where it was allowed.

Where most child stars complain about losing their childhoods working before the camera, acting seems to have provided the only bright moments of Blake's youth. He has memories of watching Spencer Tracy and Gene Kelly do what they did best, and he worked with such legendary actors as Humphrey Bogart and John Garfield.

In *Treasure of the Sierra Madre* (1948), Blake played a Mexican boy who sells Bogart's character the winning lottery ticket. Blake remembered Bogart insisting on eye contact during scenes and telling him he didn't like people who talked too much, messed up their lines, or got in the way.

Blake played John Garfield's character as a boy in *Humoresque* (1946). "I had a difficult scene to play, and I couldn't pull it off. And John Garfield cleared the room and said, 'Robert, remember this for the rest of your life. Your life is the rehearsal. Your performance is real.' There's nobody who could say that more truthfully than me. I found an audience when I was two years old, and they never left me."[91]

Blake, with his dark hair and big, soulful brown eyes, was often cast as Latin characters and played a Native American boy, Little Beaver, in the *Red Ryder* series. Baby pictures of his daughter Rosie reveal a striking resemblance to her father.

In 1950 Blake joined the army and returned to acting on television in the mid-1950s. He turned down the role of Little Joe in *Bonanza* to act in films such as *Pork Chop Hill* (1959) and *The Purple Gang* (1960). Blake gave fine performances in *Tell Them Willie Boy is Here* (1969), *Electra Guide in Blue* (1973), and a 1981 TV version of *Of Mice and Men*. Often he helped with writing, producing, and directing with no screen credit.

---

[91]   Blake, Robert. *Tales of a Rascal.* Black Rainbow Publications, 2011.

Natalie Wood and Robert Blake in This Property is Condemned
(1966) © Paramount—Silver Screen Cinema Collection

Blake was broke in 1965 with a small family, his wife Sondra Kerr and his baby son Noah. His good friend Natalie Wood got him a part in *This Property is Condemned*. As often ironically happened in Wood's films, she was forced to do a scene in the water and was terrified. Blake stayed under the water, holding her up to help alleviate her fears.

His greatest performance was as killer Perry Smith in Truman Capote's *In Cold Blood* (1967). This has been the definitive role of Blake's career so far. The monologue where the character of Perry Smith, right before his hanging, talks about his complicated relationship with his father in front of a window with rain pouring down, was Blake's best piece of work. He has said that he used his own feelings of love and hate for his own father in that scene.

Blake is most famous for his role as colorful TV detective Tony Baretta who had a pet cockatoo named Fred in the 1970s. It's a role he wished he had never taken. In 1996 in an interview with Tom Snyder, Blake elaborated on the best and worst things he'd done for his career.

"The best thing I've ever done from my career was to allow my own soul to come out and be the artist I was born to be…because that's all I am. I don't know how to be a father, I don't know how to be a friend, but I know how to create.

"The worst thing I ever did for myself was *Baretta*. That was probably the worst mistake, the most self-destructive thing I ever did. I had *Willie Boy*, I did *Electra Guide*, I did *Cold Blood*. I was considered by the *English Press* in England one of the ten best actors in the world. Then I went and did *Baretta*. You do a series to become a film actor, or you do it when your career is over. You don't do it when you're in the middle of working with the greatest directors in the world and working on important projects.

*Lobby Card from In Cold Blood starring
Robert Blake (1967) © Columbia Pictures—
Silver Screen Cinema Collection*

"Every once in a while, in my life, my soul—little Mickey—the guy who walked on the stage and said I can say that—every once in a while that comes through and when it does, then I can do anything."[92]

Blake's last really good role was in *Judgment Day: The John List Story* (1993). Blake gave a subdued, brilliant performance as the very tightly wound mass murderer John List who killed his entire family, moved,

---

[92]   *The Late, Late Show,* Tom Snyder (Host), CBS, "Robert Blake", 1996.

remarried and assumed another identity for eighteen years before being apprehended by the police.

"John List…he doomed himself," explained Blake to *E! True Hollywood Story*. "I think that's what always happens when you kill somebody. It doesn't make any difference who you kill, you really kill yourself."

Blake's greatest roles were in films based on true crime. And then life imitated art when the actor became involved in the first huge celebrity crime story of the twenty-first century.

Actor John Solari (Photo by Amy D'Allessandro.
Courtesy of John Solari)

The Events Leading Up to May 4, 2001

John Solari, the actor who co-starred in Blake's last film to date, *Lost Highway* (1997), became a close friend of Blake's following the completion of the film. He lived in Blake's guesthouse for three months before Bonny Lee Bakley moved in and was privy to activity in the Blake house prior to the murder. Blake confided in Solari, who was the only person to stand up for him during the trial, with the exception of Blake's bodyguard Earle Caldwell. Caldwell was charged with conspiracy to commit murder. The charges against Caldwell were dropped.

Solari, an intense actor somewhat reminiscent of Sterling Hayden, is usually cast as a killer as he was in *Dark Streets* (2008) or as the man on the grassy knoll in *Ruby* (1992). In Brian DePalma's *The Black Dahlia* (2008), he had a pivotal role as a pimp with much of his dialogue improvised. Solari, who had his hair bleached blonde at the time of our interview laughed, "This time they've got me playing a German killer."[93]

As a young man in New York, Solari had a chance to become an actor. "Instead of picking up a script, I picked up the gun. I wanted to be a gangster more than an actor at the time. I didn't care about acting. Acting was a good way to get laid. They told me to go to Lee Strasberg's Actor's Studio back then," explained Solari, who has an appealing raspy voice that any actor playing a mob guy would like to have. Solari ended up doing hard time in Sing Sing and Attica on and off for sixteen years.

"I was arrested by the Seven Ups," explained Solari. ("Seven Years and Up"—a squad of plainclothes cops who used unorthodox methods of nabbing members of organized crime). "A rat gave me up. I've been legit now for a lot of years. And I respect my friends in New York and Cleveland. I've never put them down, and I never will. I come from that old school. A lot of these wise guys today…they never earned it. Their fathers are bosses and all that and they're brought in. As soon as the shit hit the fan, the bitch came right out of all of these people. They started ratting. They want to be tough guys until they have to show up. And I wasn't brought up that way. Whatever happens, you do the time."

When Solari was released from prison in 1985, he auditioned for the Actors Studio, sealing the fate that was meant for him years ago when he took a wrong turn. "You have to audition to get in. You get in on your talent…not anything else. Martin Landau, Sydney Pollack, and Mark Russell were the judges when I auditioned…a lot of good people. That's the thing I'm most proud of I did in my life," explained Solari who is now a lifetime member of the Actors Studio and the host of the outstanding cable and web-based series *The Method Actor Speaks*.

---

[93] All John Solari quotes are from an interview with the author in January 2013.

Robert Blake and Bonny Lee Bakley met at the jazz club Chadney's located across the street from NBC studios in Burbank. Bakley had stalked Blake, learning his habits and where he hung out and even asked one of his friends for his phone number who suggested that she get it herself.

Solari remembers that Blake told him about his first meeting with Bakley where they instantaneously had sex in the parking lot. "*Madone...*he did it to her three times in the back of the van. Bonny set him up. He was lonely. And men think with their...they don't think normally."

After the casual sex relationship with Blake began, Bakley continued with her mail order sex business and continued to date Christian

Robert Blake and Bonny Lee Bakley, during their April 2001 vacation in Sequoia National Park, CA, was released Monday, May 14, 2001, in Los Angeles by Blake's attorney Harland Braun. (AP Photo/Harland Braun, File) AP 2001

Brando. She told Blake she was taking birth control pills, when in reality she was taking fertility drugs.

Bakley used to tape her telephone conversations. Blake was furious when he found out she was pregnant and demanded that she have an abortion. The tapes reveal the following:

"Deliberately getting pregnant is wrong," said Blake on the recordings. "Writing letters to me about how you are going to get an abortion. You promised me. You said, 'I'll take pills. You don't have to worry, if I ever get pregnant, I swear on my life I'll get an abortion.' How can you lie to me like that?" he screamed. "Getting pregnant, deliberately lying to me about abortions. That's who you are and that's what you do and that's the name of that tune! The one thing you knew I was terrified of was anybody getting pregnant, and you did it deliberately. Why? Not because you wanted to be with me. It has something to do with some crazy shit that you want Robert Blake's baby. And that's all on you baby, and you have to live with that. You schemed this whole thing!"[94]

Probably in no small part due to Blake's reaction to the pregnancy, Bakley at first told Christian Brando he was the father.

"I mean, she tried to hustle Christian Brando," Blake told Piers Morgan. "She named my baby Christian Brando, and I changed the name. When I found out I was the father, what better thing could I do than marry her mother? What's the downside? What's the worst that can happen? In three or four years, if it didn't work out, we'd get divorced. I'd have my baby all the time with me rather than having to fly wherever she chose to live."

A DNA test confirmed that Blake was the father of Rosie; however, he has said that the minute he saw a photo of the baby he knew she was his. As vehemently as Blake insisted on the abortion, once he knew that child was his, he became a protective, extremely loving father.

John Solari remembers that Blake was furious about how Bakley had set him up, that he had a lot of anger, and was very worried about Rosie. "He loved that kid. He really did love Rosie. He used to sing to her and carry her around the house. He was afraid if his wife kept her she would turn out like the other daughters…that she might get involved in the sex business."

One of Bakley's clients, a college student from Taiwan, had paid her thousands of dollars over a period of time. Bakley took her sister and daughter with her to visit him in Irvine, California. In 1995 Bakley told the FBI that she, her sister Margerry, and thirteen-year-old daughter Holly had "dated" the student in the summer of 1994. Bakley was now prostituting her own child.[95]

---

[94]   *E! True Hollywood Story*, "Robert Blake," "E" Entertainment Television Network, April 28, 2002

[95]   McDougal, Dennis and Mary Murphy. *Blood Cold: Fame Sex and Murder in Hollywood*, New York: Onyx, 2002.

"He was protective over the baby because Bonny was like a hooker. He didn't want Rosie to become a hooker. Or get involved in child pornography. I wouldn't have put it past her to do that. I used to call her family Jerry Springer rejects," said Solari, who also mentioned that Bakley had been talking about moving the family into Blake's house.

Solari, who moved out of the guesthouse at the time Bakley was moving in, said he saw suitcases of Bakley's pornographic material.

"I remember I felt really bad for him. I felt really sorry for him," said Solari about Blake. "He told me all this stuff about Bonny. He had to marry her to keep the kid. I thought this man is in so much pain. I would have done anything for the guy. And he was Italian, so you gotta help him. I remember we were just sitting there, and he showed me all these boxes she had sent ahead. It was unbelievable the stuff she had…the letters, the pornography. She was going back into the business, even though she was married to him. I could have put an ice pick in her eyeball. I couldn't stand her."

Solari was in Cleveland doing a radio show at the time of Bakley's murder. He heard about it on television.

"The Los Angeles cops, including Detective Ron Ito, came there. They said they wanted to talk to me. I said I don't talk to cops without a lawyer. Ito or his partner said to me, 'Only guilty people need a lawyer.' I said that only stupid people talk without a lawyer. That trip was a waste. I wasn't going to say anything,"

Earle Caldwell, Blake's bodyguard, talked about a guy with a buzz cut hanging around the house, possibly stalking Bakley.

"It's a true story; somebody was hanging around the house. Back where she lived. There was somebody following her. She talked about that to Robert," revealed Solari.

During Blake's preliminary hearing, stuntmen Gary McLarty and Ronald Duffy Hambleton claimed Blake tried to hire them to kill his wife. It turns out one of these men thought he saw spaceships and thought that his wife bugged his motorcycle, and the other was also known to have drug-induced hallucinations. Naturally, they were discredited.

In May of 2005, Sondra Kerr Blake, Blake's wife of more than twenty years and mother of Noah and Delinah Blake, testified in a deposition for the civil case against Robert Blake. She stated that Bernard Kowalski, producer of *Baretta,* his wife Helen, and others told her that Blake was attempting to take a contract out on her life and that of her lover actor Steve Railsback. At this time, Railsback and Kerr were filming the movie *Helter Skelter* (1976) about the Manson family.

My source, who was a very good friend of Bernard Kowalski, told this author that he had heard that Blake was allegedly soliciting stuntmen and crew on the set of *Baretta* to kill his first wife.

"That never came out in the criminal trial," said Solari of Sondra Kerr Blake's deposition. Solari also mentioned that at one time Railsback had been cast to play Robert Blake in a TV biopic, which has not been made as of the date of this writing. "That was payback, I think," smiled Solari.

"One reason I stood up for Robert Blake was that it didn't make sense to me that he would go to stuntmen to do a hit," explained Solari. "Why would he go to them when he and I were friends hanging out? He knew my background. You know what I'm saying? If anyone I knew had had anything to do with this, you would have never found her. She would have been a cactus plant. I don't think Blake had the *cajones* to do it himself. And this thing about leaving the gun in the restaurant…it's so outrageous it's got to be true. *If* he orchestrated this thing, I think he did it for the kid. Definitely. That's the only reason, if he did it. The truth is, I believe she was being followed because of that business of hers."

John Solari and Robert Blake had a falling out during the time of the criminal trial. Solari was the only person who stood up for Blake at the time of the arrest. "And he didn't appreciate that. People used to come to the court to support him, and he'd tell them not to come. But he could never control me. I was his friend and wouldn't let him treat me like the hired help.

"Blake knew that *if* I knew anything, I would go to my grave with it. It got back to me from Blake's private investigator that he was talking behind my back like I was the bad guy…because I was on TV. My Italian friends in Cleveland and New York knew what I was trying to do. I was trying to help him.

"He got rid of me by having me put on the witness list. He ignored me and barred me from the court. That's how they got me out of there. Blake doesn't know what friendship is. He's a Hollywood guy who knows how to use people. I just realized that the guy has talent, but he's not a decent human being. You know what I'm saying? Talent doesn't make you a good guy. When Blake reads what you write, he will make his fans think I'm the bad guy, but Robert and I know the truth.

"Shellie Samuels, the DA, was really good. I felt bad for her. I remember one day I told her, 'I'm rooting for you.' She said, '*You* are rooting for me?' She couldn't believe it."

Just as in the case of O. J. Simpson, Robert Blake was found not guilty in the criminal trial, yet found liable in the civil case for $30 million. This judgment was later reduced, and Blake declared bankruptcy.

"Nothing that man did made sense," said Solari. "I knew he would lose the civil case as soon as he opened his mouth. Blake really thought he was going to win that case."

Delinah Blake, who is now a psychologist, adopted her little sister and is raising Rose Lenore Sophia Blake, along with her husband, as her daughter. A 2012 tabloid ran a picture of Rose with Delinah and her daughter Natalie. Rose looks like a happy pre-teen. The article alluded to the fact that Rose no longer has contact with her father because Delinah thought it was better that way.

This beautiful child who came from damaged people now has a chance. Rose's parents each endured their own horrific abuses as children, and by all appearances Rose is a happy, well-adjusted young girl living a normal family life.

Robert Blake reacts the moment he is found "not guilty" at the criminal trial on March 16, 2005. © Nick Ut/Reuters/Pool/Corbis © Corbis

On a 2012 episode of *Dr. Phil,* Blake revealed his innermost feelings to Dr. Phil McGraw, "When you wonder what the hell you're doing alive, when everything has been taken away from you. When you find out your friends were your enemies and your family were worse enemies. And they had you sign a whole bunch of shit and they stole everything. There's no worse betrayal in the world than the betrayal of people you love and trust. It wasn't losing anything that broke my heart. What broke my heart was losing the people that took it. When you find out they didn't love you. And they had their hand in your pocket the whole time. That's what made me want to die after the criminal trial.

"I'm still hurt. The only thing that will cure that hurt is if I can get back on that bull that bucked me off and ride him. If I can get out in front of the camera making the most beautiful film I ever made. That's all I really want from life."[96]

---

96 *Dr. Phil,* "Robert Blake: The Man behind the Murder Headlines," Syndicated, September 20, 2012

CHAPTER 12

The Real Mickey Cohen

Mickey Cohen, Hollywood's most legendary gangster, right, and Jim Smith, left, who Cohen once said was his "indispensable" right-hand-man (Courtesy of Jim Smith)

Mickey Cohen, the most powerful west coast mobster of the mid-1940s and 1950s, was short in stature but made up for it with a larger than life presence that resonates to this day. Watch any of his televised interviews and his candor and humor shines through…Mickey Cohen had charisma in spades.

Cohen was as much of a celebrity as any of the popular actors of his time and while maybe not as good looking, was at least as debonair. Cohen cut quite the dashing figure, with his impeccably tailored suits; perfectly shined shoes; the ubiquitous gleaming pinky ring whether diamond, ruby, or emerald; and the scent of English Lavender cologne that preceded him into every room and remained long after he was gone. He was loved by the public—quite unusual for an underworld figure and would stand for hours signing autographs, never refusing anyone. One reason for the public's affection for him was that not every headline about Cohen was considered all that bad. In one case, he was considered something of a vigilante hero.

Captain Harry Lorenson of the Los Angeles Police Department had heard of a sixty-three-year-old widow named Mrs. Phillips. The widow failed to pay an $8.09 radio repair bill. Alfred Pearson, of the Sky Radio Shop, through legal proceedings, obtained title to Mrs. Phillips's $4,000.00 home for $26.50 over the nonpayment of this miniscule radio bill. Lorenson, who had arrested the unscrupulous Pearson previously, must have been frustrated by the lack of what the police could do about this man's continued abuse of his customers. He reportedly asked Cohen for help. Pearson was beaten up badly by Cohen's men who were dubbed the "seven dwarfs" by the press. He and his men were arrested. Cohen quickly paid the bond for his men and made sure the home was returned to Mrs. Phillips along with some money. He was in many ways considered a Robin Hood to the community. Following the notoriety of this case, newspaper czar William Randolph Hearst instructed his reporters to stop calling Cohen a gangster and instead refer to him as a gambler.

It was very important to Cohen to be liked. "He did his best to be liked, which wasn't a stretch for him. With women, especially, he went out of his way. He put them on a pedestal and would try to be the ultimate gentleman. He often said he knew he wasn't very good looking, but he tried to be neat and clean and a gentleman. He did everything he could to personify that behavior. He also had a theory that the reason he had never been convicted of any crime in California was because people liked him. And he thought if you were nice to everybody, that person might be on a jury or know somebody on a jury, and he thought it might help,"[97] laughed Jim Smith, Mickey Cohen's associate, in an interview with this author.

In Cohen's 1975 autobiography, *In My Own Words,* he wrote, "In the car when someone drives me right now, I say, 'Look it, you give every son-of-a-bitch on the street the right-of-way even if they don't deserve it and don't ask no questions. I don't want nobody seeing me sitting in the car that cuts into nobody, because when you go before a jury of twelve, you can never tell who may be sitting on that jury. It may be one of the persons driving in the other car who is on one of the juries.'" [98]

"Mickey was one of the smartest guys I ever knew," said Smith, who met Cohen at the age of seventeen when he was just starting out as a fighter. Boxing was something the two men had in common. Neither Smith nor Cohen smoked or drank, and they both loved ice cream. One of Cohen's favorite pastimes was to get on a train with professional fighters and spend days talking boxing with them.

Later, Jim Smith became Cohen's right-hand man and constant companion, staying with him from the time he was released from his second stint in prison for tax evasion in 1972 until his death from cancer in 1976.

Cohen's job in prison was to give out tools to inmates. While he waited for an inmate to come in, he'd watch television. A psychopathic inmate who had no associations with the mob, Berl Estes McDonald, snuck up behind Cohen while he was watching television and beat him nearly to death with a lead pipe. Cohen had brain surgery where the portions of his brain that controlled his lower extremities were removed. He was in a coma

---

[97]   All Jim Smith quotes from multiple interviews with the author during 2012 and 2013.

[98]   The majority of Mickey Cohen quotes are from Cohen, Mickey, and John Peer Nugent. *Mickey Cohen: In My Own Words* as told to John Peer Nugent, Englewood Cliffs, New Jersey: Prentice Hall International, Inc., 1975.

for twenty-one days and was left partially paralyzed. Smith told this author, "I was Mickey's legs."

Smith, who is polished, articulate, and charming, spent decades as Cohen's friend and confidante and knew him better than anyone.

Cohen, who had a third grade education and whose grammar was lacking, has been erroneously portrayed in books and films as somewhat dim-witted. Smith found him to be just the opposite.

"Now he didn't know what month came after the next, and he didn't know his ABCs because he didn't have any formal education," explained Smith. "However, many times I saw him go into a room with many people...doctors, lawyers, multimillionaire businessmen, and even a former prosecutor. And when they left the room, Mickey had their money. Who was the smarter guy?"

Cohen had a talent for reading people and sizing them up for the

Jim Smith, unidentified man, Pearl Manzie, entertainer
Barbara McNair, Manzie's daughter-in-law, and
Mickey Cohen (Courtesy of Jim Smith)

potential score. Despite his reputation for largesse and leaving huge tips, he also knew how to keep an eye on his own money.

"I remember we were in a restaurant one time with fourteen or fifteen people who were Mickey's guests," remembers Smith. "I'm sitting at the opposite end of the table. Mickey motioned me to come over to him. He said, 'Something is wrong with the bill.' Now I was already shocked because I wouldn't have any idea what the bill was. Of course, I wasn't watching or paying attention. It surprised me that he would know something about the bill. He asked me very politely to ask the waiter what was wrong with the bill. So I asked; it turned out that one of the people who was Mickey's invited guest saw some friends of his and told the waiter to put their bill on Mickey's check. This guy wanted to be a big shot and pick up his friend's tab, but he wanted to put it on Mickey's check. Mickey spotted that. It was amazing to me that he would know. He could figure out that the bill was a couple of hundred more than it should be. He wasn't exactly the idiot or moron they want to portray him to be."

Smith appeared on the Mickey Cohen episode of *Rogue's Gallery* in 1998. A policeman from the LAPD Gangster Squad also appeared on the show. He proudly told the story of putting a bug in Cohen's television set and how stupid Cohen was for tipping five dollars each time the TV repairman showed up to change the batteries in the recorder.

"He made a big deal out of the fact that they bugged Mickey's TV set in his home," elaborates Smith. "These cops listened to the tapes, and they thought they were really *learning* something. Mickey knew the bug was there the whole time. Now, first of all, Mickey had Jim Vaus around at that time, and he was an electronics expert. He swept Mickey's house all the time and knew if there were bugs there or not. The cops thought Mickey was dumb, and Mickey thought the cops were stupid. He left the bug there. He said what he wanted the cops to hear. The Gangster Squad… how many arrests did they make? None.

"Mickey had a lot of philosophies, but he often said that nothing was too good for a friend or too bad for an enemy," explains Smith. "If he really liked somebody, there's nothing he wouldn't do for them. Money, presents, or anything they wanted. He'd help them if they had a problem…try to work it out for them. If he considered somebody a friend, he'd do anything for them.

"On the other hand, if somebody was an enemy, there wasn't anything bad enough he could do, either. If he had to take their life, he'd take their life. But he never took innocent people's lives. If they were supposed to be part of the racket world, and they did something wrong, and it called for that, that's what he would do.

"Mickey had many facets to him. People thought he was this sadistic killer. And every book about him only talks about the shootings, the killings, the mob, bombs blowing up, machine guns, and all that kind of stuff. I'm not trying to whitewash it, that was part of Mickey's life too, but it wasn't all of it.

"People think if Mickey or anyone else is a gangster, that they're a gangster twenty-four-hours a-day," explains Smith. "They think that gangsters have no sense of humor. That they're always murderers and kill people

Mickey Cohen and Jim Smith as young professional fighters—Photo Compilation (Courtesy of Jim Smith)

and that they're always sadistic, sour, mean, and corrupt. Nothing could be further from the truth. You take any so-called gangster, and it's just like a job to him. He has moments when he does what he does for money. But when that's done, he goes home to his wife or girlfriend. He may have children, and he has emotions. Sometimes they go to church and are very civic-minded.

"In the old days, the *Mustache Petes* used to have a legitimate business," continued Smith. "And they would be considered pillars of the community. But then in quiet, they would be running some kind of mafia activity. So it's only a portion of their lives, just like any legitimate person goes to work eight hours a day. When they come home, they have dinner with their loving family. They have friends and go to social events. And that's what it is…it's not a twenty-four-hour-a-day existence."

The Early Years

Cohen was born in the Brownsville section of Brooklyn, New York, in 1911, 1913, or 1914. The record of his birth is missing. His father Max died when he was sixteen days old. His mother Fanny moved with Mickey, his three older brothers, and his two sisters to Boyle Heights in Los Angeles, which was considered Russian Town and a ghetto neighborhood.

A struggling single mother with a family to feed, widow Fanny Cohen opened up a Mom and Pop grocery store. One of Mickey's earliest memories was keeping himself occupied by stacking the cans on the shelves.

"When I got into hustling, I wasn't even six," wrote Cohen. "My older brothers, Louie and Harry, used to take me to hustle the old *Los Angeles Record* on the corner of Soto and Brooklyn Streets. They would set me up on a stack of newspapers, which at the time were two cents. I'd just sit there on the papers, and whoever would come along would just put two cents in my hand and kid with me and take the paper. They tell me I was a very, very bashful child and would hardly open my mouth. I would have been better off staying that way today."

Cohen often frequented pool halls rather than going to school. He recalled that when he was seven or eight years old, people would leave pieces of paper with him. He couldn't read but figured out that these papers contained bets. During prohibition, they would leave packages with him, and he'd get a quarter when the packages containing whiskey were picked up.

"Mickey was pretty much left in the care of his older brother Harry who was a gambler. He worked deals and was kind of a promoter. Harry wasn't exactly in the underworld, but he wasn't exactly legitimate either," said Smith.

To keep him out of the poolrooms, his mother tried to enroll Cohen in a Hebrew school. "Mickey always got into fights, and he liked to flip the lights on and off. The rabbi came out and said 'Who is bothering those lights?' Anyway they kicked him out of there in a couple of days. His childhood was spent in and out of reform schools, and he sold newspapers. Mickey was very smart streetwise," explained Smith. "He knew how to fight, how to get corners, and how to make money. He always had a big roll of cash because he would save his money."

Cohen ran away at the age of fifteen to Cleveland, Ohio, to box.

"Mickey was a Jew, but in the mob, he was raised by Italians. He was kind of turned out in the mob by Italians. He went to Cleveland, where his brother Harry lived, to become a fighter," said Smith. In addition to fighting, Cohen was also doing heists.

"Mickey didn't realize he was holding up places run by Italians. He was holding up nightclubs and gambling places. Finally, they waited for him, trapped him, and brought him in to speak to these Italians who were running everything. And he had to stop. He knew if he didn't stop, he'd be killed," elaborates Smith. "The Italians liked him, felt sorry for him, and took him under their wing. And they had Mickey work for them. He didn't have to pull holdups anymore. He was brought into the mob by the Italians and worked for them. He was friendly with Jews, but he became part and parcel of the Italian mob. He learned a lot of Italian ways and loved Italian food. So he really learned how to behave himself, how to act and dress like Italians. He learned all his method of operations from the Italians."

Cohen recalled his days with the Italians in Cleveland in his autobiography. He remembered living with the families, hiding out in their cellars when necessary, and being referred to as the "Jew kid," which he didn't mind because the name Mickey Cohen was hard for them to remember or say with their broken English.

"There was an Italian kid named Jimmy Yale. We used to call him One-Arm, because he only had one. He was very close to me, like a brother. His mother once hid me out from the coppers with a beef," wrote Cohen.

"When they came and asked about me, she yelled out, 'I gotta no Jew kid here.' They said they were going to bust the door down. She put a shotgun out on the second story window and said, 'You breaka my door and I'ma killa you all.' And I'm there waiting for her to finish making the marinara sauce for our spaghetti dinner. So naturally I'm going to pick up a lot of Italian ways."

While in Chicago, Cohen caught the favorable attention of Al Capone. He remembered being called into his office and in a state of awe being told he did a good job by Capone.

"And then he did something that was a very big thing for me—he kind of held my head and kissed me on both cheeks. After that meeting, it was kind of like a whole new world for me," remembered Cohen. "People who never knew me before, knew me now. I wasn't just a punk kid any more. I was someone who had done something to justify the favor of Al Capone."

In addition to Al Capone, Cohen also admired Frank Costello. "Capone was making $12 million a month in the 1920s when most people couldn't even eat," explained Smith with his smooth, baritone voice suitable for broadcasting. "Mickey was partners with Mattie Capone and Ralph Capone, Al's younger brothers. So Mickey knew the whole family pretty well. He was just a young kid, and he was on the lower, lower echelon of the criminal world, and Al Capone was like the superstar.

"And Frank Costello, they called him the prime minister of the underworld. Costello came along later, in the 1940s. Those were really the top two. When Lucky Luciano was deported, Frank Costello took over the whole area. He was running New York. He was really the top guy. And he was a gentleman, a very elegant dresser, and he was everything Mickey would admire."

*Ben Siegel and George Raft in 1944 (Copyright
Bettmann/Corbis/AP Images) AP 2011*

Los Angeles and Ben "Bugsy" Siegel

With his wavy dark hair and piercing blue eyes, Benjamin Siegel was as
handsome as any movie star. As a teenager on the lower east side of New
York, he befriended Meyer Lansky who was later known as the mob's
accountant. Lansky along with Charles "Lucky" Luciano were later responsible for organizing crime into a national syndicate by killing the *Moustache
Petes* (old time Sicilian gangsters whose time had passed), most notably Joe
"The Boss" Masseria in 1931. Siegel was reportedly one of the four hit men
hired for that job.

Murder, Incorporated was established following the National Crime
Syndicate by Albert Anastasia and Louis "Lepke" Buchalter. Members Ben
Siegel and Meyer Lansky also helped form Murder, Inc.

Siegel despised the nickname Bugsy that was reportedly given to him
because of his explosive temper, and slang for that at the time was "going
bugs." "My friends call me Ben, strangers call me Mr. Siegel, and guys I
don't like call me Bugsy but not to my face."

In 1936, Frank Costello and Lucky Luciano sent Ben Siegel to Los Angeles because Jack Dragna wasn't doing that well, and they felt Los Angeles had the potential to be bigger and that Ben Siegel was suited to do the job. And eventually the bosses in Cleveland and Chicago sent Cohen to work with Ben Siegel. "They wanted me on the coast with Benny—to have somebody stand in for their end of the action. I do have a little suspicion that they wanted somebody to be with Benny like me from Ohio, anyway" wrote Cohen.

When Cohen first came to Los Angeles, he didn't see Siegel right away. He enjoyed visiting his family and did some freelance robberies on his own without consulting Siegel, who demanded a kick back.

"Mickey liked Ben. He saw him as a mentor. At first they weren't really close because Ben wanted him to kick some money back from a robbery," said Smith. "Mickey wouldn't have kicked back money to his own grandmother. There have been phony stories that he did kick back the money. But he wouldn't have had the right to do that because there were two other guys on that robbery and he couldn't give back their money. They risked life and liberty for their shares and they had already divided up the cash."

Eventually Cohen and Siegel made peace with one another. "After Mickey started working for Ben, he liked Ben's ways, the way he dressed, and he was smooth. Mickey saw him as a mentor. Ben Siegel had been around top people and Mickey hadn't," said Smith. "Mickey had been pretty much a rough hustler and hold-up guy up to that point. He learned a lot of finer things from Ben. He looked up to him and admired him. Ben was nearly ten years older than Mickey and had been around Luciano and Lansky and all those other people."

Siegel's mistress, leggy, brunette beauty Virginia Hill, is one of the most notorious gun molls of the twentieth century. Born in Alabama and raised in Georgia, this Southern belle had sass and a sharp tongue, as evidenced by her testimony before the Kefauver committee in the 1950s. Hill and Siegel had a tempestuous relationship, alternately fighting and loving. Siegel used to call her his "flamingo," and she called him "baby blue eyes." However, there was one person who didn't care for Hill at all.

"Mickey knew Virginia Hill very well. He couldn't stand her. She talked down to him. Mickey didn't like her; he thought she was nuts. Virginia's car had broken down and was being serviced. She only drove Cadillac's. Ben didn't drive a Cadillac; he drove a Buick, which wasn't good enough for her. She insisted on borrowing a Cadillac, so Ben had Mickey give her his Cadillac. So Virginia borrowed it, and Mickey didn't like that anyway because he was very sensitive about people touching his stuff," laughed Smith. "Virginia leaves the car somewhere, and someone stole it while she was out. Mickey doesn't report it because he doesn't believe in reporting things to the police. So for about thirty days, nothing happens. The police finally find Mickey's Cadillac. Apparently, she left the key in the ignition, and some drunken sailor stole it. The police come and bother Mickey. They want to know why he didn't report it. Mickey said he doesn't report things to the police. No, he never did like Virginia Hill at all."

Siegel enjoyed Hollywood and befriended many stars such as Clark Gable, Gary Cooper, Cary Grant, Jean Harlow, and her stepfather Marino Bello. Harlow was godmother to Siegel's daughter Millicent. Siegel and his wife Esta also had another daughter named Barbara.

One of Siegel's Hollywood friends was George Raft, whom he knew from New York. "They always try to make out that George Raft and Ben were childhood friends. Well, they weren't because Raft was older than Siegel," says Smith. "He might have known him because Raft traveled back and forth from California to New York. When Ben came out here, he got very friendly with Raft, and so did Mickey. They like to write that Raft was a gangster because he played them in the movies. When mobster Owney Madden left New York and went to Hot

Ben Siegel and mistress Virginia Hill—Photo Compilation, Historical Editorial Archive

Springs, Arkansas, Raft used to drive for him. But he was never a hoodlum or mob guy. He just played those roles.

"When Ben came out here, everyone thought he and Raft were really close friends. They weren't. He liked being around Mickey and Ben because he loved being around tough guys. Raft would do things with Ben and Mickey. He went to Ben's house for dinner and Mickey's house for dinner. They hung around quite a bit, but it was all nothing stuff. They would go to the fights together and go to horseraces. Raft used to get his clothes from Mickey's tailor.

"There was one time when Raft and Ben went to Alan Smiley's apartment at the Sunset Towers. They were phoning in bets. And somehow the police got wind of it, and they came up and arrested Smiley and Ben. They booked them on bookmaking charges, but actually they were just placing bets," explained Smith. "And Raft is trying to get arrested. He said, 'If you're arresting them, then you've got to arrest me.' But they wouldn't arrest Raft because he was an actor. They were just trying to roust Ben and Smiley. So they took them to jail but wouldn't take Raft. He went to court to testify for Ben, but the charges were all dismissed anyway.

"Ben liked Raft, but he used him to be introduced to the movie stars. Ben wanted to be in that circle with those wealthy legitimate people. In 1940 Ben borrowed $100,000.00 off Raft. Now Raft thought he was loaning it to him, but Ben was never going to pay it back. So Ben used Raft in that spot. But Raft didn't know that he got clipped for money because he was a sucker.

"Finally, when Raft was sixty-five years old he got arrested for income tax evasion. And everybody thought he was going to drop dead of a heart attack he was so scared. And nothing happened to him; they gave him a pass. He was a nice guy and gave a lot of money away to different people. And he ended up broke because he blew all his money. He accredited that to fast women and slow horses," laughed Smith. "He was a sucker for the horse races. He just liked to be around hoodlums and racket guys. It gave him a feeling of superiority and toughness that he wanted to personify."

Cohen had a former partner from Chicago, Benny "The Meatball" Gamson. Gamson came out to California hoping that Cohen could get him in with Siegel and Johnny Roselli.

"Benny was called 'The Meatball' because he looked like a little meatball," wrote Cohen. "Benny was a little, arrogant, moody kind of guy, not easy to like. Even Mattie Capone didn't like him."

Cohen didn't feel that Gamson had the class to work with Siegel and the others. The nicer Cohen tried to be about letting Gamson down, the more belligerent he became. Gamson started saying that he didn't need anyone and started going out on his own. He grabbed a sickly, meek, likable bookie named Barber Brown in Cohen's hometown Boyle Heights.

"Benny knew that I liked Brown very well and that it would be kind of a slap in the face to me to grab this fellow," said Cohen. Gamson abused Barber, and Cohen admitted in his book to shooting at him to make the point that his patience was growing weak.

Cohen stopped there in the story with his co-author John Peer Nugent because there is no statute of limitations on murder.

"Mickey did kill several people, but those were people he was at war with," said Smith. "He killed a guy named Meatball Gamson because Meatball struck him from behind with a lead pipe once. Meatball tried to kill Mickey, and Mickey didn't kill him at that time, but he killed him later. Because it was war."

There was also the killing of Max Shaman. In 1945 Cohen owned a restaurant and sporting joint called the La Brea Club. His associate Hooky Rothman got into an altercation with the Shaman brothers.

"A lot of books make out that Mickey murdered this guy named Maxie Shaman. They got the story all wrong. The Shaman brothers were hoodlums themselves. They weren't pillars of the community," elaborates Smith. "As a matter of fact, they were in Mickey's gambling house, and the one Shaman brother got beat up for causing trouble.

"The next day Maxie came busting into Mickey's office hollering and screaming. He pulled a gun on Mickey, what he didn't know was that Mickey had a gun he could take out quickly. And when Maxie was going to shoot Mickey, Mickey shot Maxie first and killed him."

As was the case with Hollywood stars who found themselves in trouble, the cry went out to "Get Geisler"—Jerry Geisler, the most sought-after attorney for celebrities.

"Geisler told Mickey not to worry about anything," said Smith. "Mickey just had to get him $25,000.00 that night and not to worry about it. So Mickey got him the money, and the case was handled. The verdict was self-defense."

In 1945, with the very capable Mickey Cohen handling the Los Angeles interests, Siegel turned his attention toward Las Vegas, Nevada, which was then just basically desert, and the construction of the Flamingo Hotel. Siegel had brought the project to the attention of Meyer Lansky and the eastern syndicate. Siegel had dreams of building a gambling Mecca that would be legal, at least on the surface, in Nevada. The syndicate agreed to fund the project, which was budgeted at $1.5 million.

Siegel became obsessed with making the hotel the finest it could be, ordering the best materials from the black market during postwar shortages. Ironically, Siegel was conned himself when dishonest contractors began selling him material by day, taking it away at night, and then reselling it back to him the next day. Siegel quickly exceeded his budget.

By 1946 the costs were more than $4 million, and in 1947 they were in excess of $6 million. Siegel's checks began to bounce, and he began selling non-existent shares of the hotel to try and get out of this extreme financial trouble. One day his temper got the best of him, and he threatened to kill some people at the construction site of the hotel. Seeing the frightened look on his head contractor's face, Siegel said, "Don't worry, we only kill each other."

Not only were funds being mismanaged, they were also being skimmed. Some have said Siegel stole the money, and others say Hill took millions and put it in a foreign bank account.

"They've said that Virginia Hill was a spy for the Chicago Mob," said Smith. "She wasn't a spy. She really liked Ben. And Ben did not steal the money and give it to her to take to Europe. Lansky and the others were around. They wouldn't have let her handle money. They wouldn't let her be a courier and take that money out of there."

"There was no doubt in Meyer's mind," wrote Lucky Luciano in his 1975 memoir *The Testament of Lucky Luciano*, "that Bugsy had skimmed the dough from his building budget, and that he was sure that Siegel was preparing to skip as well as skim, in case the roof was going to fall in on him."[99]

In Cuba there was a meeting, and Lansky reluctantly agreed that Siegel, his childhood friend, who had stolen from them, had to go.

"The night before he was killed, Ben said to Mickey, 'I think there's some problems. Get some armament...some guns. I think I'm going to need them.' Mickey said OK," said Smith. "But he never got a chance to do it...because they killed Ben the next night.

"Mickey knew Ben was going to be killed in advance. Almost everybody in the underworld knew. Mickey didn't like it, but he knew it had to be done. Once the order comes down that somebody is going to be hit, there's nothing anyone can do about it."

While Virginia Hill was in Europe, Siegel, her brother Chick Hill, and his girlfriend Jeri Mason, were in her house on the evening of June 20, 1947.

"Chick Hill and Jeri Mason were upstairs at the time. The last book on Mickey said that Alan Smiley was in on it. He didn't know what was going to happen. He wasn't even a part of anything. Ben just liked him and let him hang around.

"You'd have to know Smiley, and I knew him very well. He was a very nervous guy," laughed Smith. "He would have never gone in there and sat on that couch when they're going to open up with a carbine rifle. As it was, a bullet went through his sleeve. It's a wonder he didn't have a heart attack right then. He didn't know any more about it than Ben did. He just sat down on the couch next to Ben, and the rifle went off."

Siegel was sitting on the couch reading a copy of the *Los Angeles Times* with his friend Smiley when a fusillade of bullets shattered the living room window. Siegel was hit with many bullets, including through the lungs and twice in the head. One shot penetrated his right cheek and exited through

[99] Gosch, Martin A., and Richard Hammer. New York: Little Brown and Company, 1975. *The Last Testament of Lucky Luciano*

the left side of his neck. The other bullet struck the right bridge of his nose where it met the right eye socket. The pressure from the bullet caused Siegel's right eye to blow out of its socket.

With Hill suspiciously absent at the time of the assassination and the murder having taken place in her own house, it's been suggested that she might have been in on it.

"Mickey said when Virginia came back from Europe she was devastated," said Smith. "She didn't know."

Decades after Siegel's death, an ex-mob associate named Eddie Cannizzaro confessed to being the triggerman in Siegel's hit.

"That guy was a nothing guy. Cannizzaro might have killed some hobo or something, but he did not kill Ben Siegel," said Smith. "They would have never used him on that. He was dying of cancer and wanted to get some notoriety or maybe try to sell a story to get some money. He didn't do anything. He was a bum on the fringes of things with Jack Dragna (who was at one time the boss of Los Angeles). He was no hitter. They would have never given him a spot like that with that important a hit. It had to be done with people who really knew their way around.

"How is it that nobody from the mob went to Ben Siegel's funeral," asked Smith rhetorically. "One of the biggest things in gangland was always to go to the funeral. There are usually many, many cars, flowers, and dignitaries from the mob. Nobody wanted to go Siegel's funeral. Nobody. Even George Raft didn't go. And why was that?"

Siegel's brother, Dr. Maurice Siegel, Ben's widow Esta, and their two young daughters were the only people at the funeral. The reason no mob figures attended the services was because of the fact that Siegel stole from the mob, and that was an extreme insult to those in the underworld. So no one connected to the mob attended.

"Frank Costello called Mickey and told him not to go," explained Smith, "which was really something because Mickey was Ben's right-hand man. And Mickey said OK. George Raft called Mickey the morning of the funeral and asked what time he was going. When Mickey said he wasn't going, Raft decided not to go. Raft was not a part of the mob but considered himself to be, and since the mob wasn't attending, he decided he wasn't going either."

Today there is no statue to Siegel who was a true visionary and began Las Vegas, which is now so much bigger than even he could have imagined. There is a small memorial plaque to Siegel at the Flamingo Las Vegas, between the pool and the wedding chapel.

In a 2012 interview with Diana Edelman, Millicent Siegel said, "My father would hate what Las Vegas is today. What corporations did for Las Vegas was never his vision of this town."[100]

The War of the Sunset Strip

No sooner was Ben Siegel killed, than the war of the Sunset Strip began. Jack Dragna, the boss of the Los Angeles crime family, barely tolerated the competition of Ben Siegel and the east coast syndicate.

Following Siegel's assassination, Cohen took over Siegel's operation and wasn't inclined to bow down to Jack Dragna's authority. "After Benny Siegel got knocked in, people like Jack Dragna kept feeling that their prestige was badly shaken," wrote Cohen. "Dragna ignored certain other people such as Frank Costello and the people in Cleveland. He went around them and declared a war."

The real start of the battle of the Sunset Strip for Cohen was when his loyal right-hand man at the time, Hooky Rothman, was killed.

"Mickey and his men had just come into his haberdashery. Mickey went right away to the bathroom to wash his hands, which he usually did," explained Smith. "And these gunmen came in right after that because they were watching him. They came to assassinate Mickey. While Mickey was in the bathroom, Hooky saw one of the guys had a shotgun; he ran over and tried to jerk the shotgun out of the guy's hands. This guy pulled both triggers and blew Hooky apart.

"Mickey could hear the shooting. And he had a gun on him that he carried all of the time. He lay down on the floor and put his foot against the

100 Edelman, Diane, "The Daughter of Las Vegas: an interview with Millicent Siegel" http://www.dtravelsround.com/2012/07/25/daughter-las-vegas-interview-millicent-siegel/

door so it wouldn't come open. He held the gun in his hand in case someone tried to come in. But nobody tried to come in the bathroom where Mickey was. They hit a guy named Jimmy Rist, shot part of his ear off, but they didn't kill him. They just wounded him. They killed Hooky because they blew him apart. This all happened on the Sunset Strip in the 1940s.

"Nobody could identify anybody in the shoot-out for the cops," wrote Cohen. "That isn't the way of the racket world. But the guys who did this, they're not around anymore."

Jim Smith explains, "Mickey killed people in the war he had with Jack Dragna. There were bodies all over the place. They killed a lot of Mickey's men, and he killed some of their men. The people that he killed…I try to explain to people…if you're going to portray yourself as part of the underworld and be with the underworld—that's fine. If you make mistakes or do the wrong thing, you've got to be punished just like in regular society. If legitimate people don't do the right thing, they get put in jail and punished. It's the same thing with the underworld. Mickey didn't go around killing innocent people. Like Ben Siegel said, 'We only kill each other.' And that's really the way it is. If people are in that world and they don't do the right thing, they can get killed or something else can happen to them."

Not long after Hooky Rothman was killed, Cohen was driving down his street in Brentwood, where he had dinner guests including George Raft waiting for him. He turned into his driveway, and all hell broke loose. They were shooting at him from both sides of the street.

"Now I think I'm best and I'm coolest in an emergency," wrote Cohen. "The minute I sensed what was happening, I fell to the floor and drove that goddamn car from San Vicente to Wilshire with one hand. That's about a mile. I probably couldn't do that again in a thousand times."

Cohen's only injury was cuts from flying glass. After things settled down, Cohen returned home with some back-up men. He said that he knew the shooters must have been Dragna's men.

"There ain't none of them around now, either. They all expired," wrote Cohen. "Naturally, when I came into the house, I was bleeding a bit from the glass, and I was also a bit disheveled. George Raft says to me, 'Jesus, what happened?' I said don't worry about what happened. Let's sit down and have dinner. He says, 'How are we going to eat dinner after this?' I said, what do ya mean, how? Get around the table and eat dinner." Nobody ate except Cohen, even though it was Raft's favorite dinner—steak and apple pie.

Another attempt on Cohen's life during the gang wars was shortly before four o'clock in the morning on July 20, 1949. Cohen was leaving Sherry's Café on Sunset Blvd. Gunmen shot at Cohen and killed his man, Neddie Herbert. Newspaper columnist Florabel Muir, starlet Dee David, an unidentified woman in the restaurant, and agent Harry Cooper, who was assigned by the attorney general to guard Cohen, were all injured. Cohen was hit in the shoulder and was the least injured of the group.

Having failed at killing Cohen by shooting him, as he seemed to have nine lives like a cat, Dragna's men bombed Cohen's home on February 6, 1950. The bomb went off shortly after four o'clock in the morning underneath Cohen's bedroom. The shock from the bomb was felt not only in

Mickey Cohen looks over damage to his wardrobe at his bombed-out house. (AP Photo 1950)

the neighborhood but as far as seven miles away. There was a vault built like a concrete bunker under Cohen's bedroom that he felt might have saved the whole house.

That night, Cohen was in his wife Lavonne's bedroom on the other side of the house. Once he knew his wife was OK, his first thought was for his little bulldog Tuffy. He ran to the bedroom to see if the dog was OK. "Well here comes Tuffy prancing out and looking at me like, 'You dirty son of a bitch, what happened?'" wrote Cohen.

Cohen was upset that half his house was blown up, but what bothered him the most was that his perfect custom tailored suits in his wardrobe were destroyed.

"The people in Brentwood wanted Mickey not to be able to stay in that neighborhood," remembered Smith. "And they did everything they could to get him out of the area after the explosion. And it had appeared in all the papers that the people in Brentwood wanted Mickey out. This was a nice, residential, high-class neighborhood. But now all of a sudden, there were shootings and bombings, and they couldn't stand it. What happened was that people from the black community had somebody put in the paper that Mickey was welcome to live in their community. They loved Mickey so much."

While Cohen was able to survive all the attempts on his life, his luck was about to end. When Cohen was brought before the Kefauver Committee, New Hampshire Senator Charles Tobey really laid into him with his questioning.

"Is it not a fact that you live extravagantly, surrounded by violence?" Senator Tobey asked Cohen.

"Whaddya mean 'surrounded by violence,'" Cohen replied. "People are shooting at *me*!"

It was Cohen's extravagant lifestyle and love affair with the media that likely made him a target of the Kefauver Committee and the IRS. They were going to make an example of him.

In 1951, based on the findings of the committee, Cohen was convicted of tax evasion and sentenced to five years in federal prison.

Cohen blamed his old mentor Ben Siegel for his situation with the IRS. Siegel once warned him, "You sonofabitch, you gotta pay your taxes." Cohen replied, "What the hell, you're gonna heist it and pay taxes on it?" He felt that the maximum time he would have done for not paying taxes at all would be a year and a day, not the four years for the first tax evasion conviction and certainly not the unprecedented fifteen-year sentence for the second conviction. A portion of Cohen's second sentence was served in Alcatraz. It was the longest sentence ever for tax evasion. Just like his mentor Al Capone, tax evasion was the only crime Cohen was ever convicted of. The government managed to do what Jack

Dragna with all his grandiose attempts on Cohen's life couldn't—get rid of Mickey but only temporarily.

During his second trial in 1961 for tax evasion there were some celebrated witnesses called to testify against Cohen.

"Jerry Lewis and Red Skelton were very close friends of Mickey's. They socialized together and Mickey went to see their performances. They went to each other's homes and everything else," explained Smith. "When Mickey got indicted in 1961 for income tax evasion, Red and Jerry were subpoenaed to appear as hostile witnesses against him. They were subpoenaed by the government to testify against him...well they didn't really testify against him. Neither one of them liked it. They were very nervous about it. Red Skelton was called first to testify. When he was on the witness stand he was kind of nervous and fidgety because that was something he wasn't used to. They were questioning him about Mickey. Anyway Red was on the witness stand about twenty or thirty minutes. He finally got off and as he was coming down off the witness stand, they called Jerry Lewis to the stand. As they passed each other, Red coming down and Jerry Lewis going to the witness chair, Jerry Lewis says to Red 'you weren't very funny up there,' and Red says back to him, 'wait until you get in front of that master of ceremonies (referring to the Judge),'" laughs Smith.

Billy Graham

When Cohen was released from prison the first time in 1956, he lived on loans from his Hollywood friends. One of his biggest benefactors was evangelist Billy Graham who paid Cohen's expenses in addition to $5,000.00 to go to a revival at Madison Square Garden where Graham expected him to come down to the stage and be baptized a Christian.

"In 1949 Billy Graham came to Los Angeles," explained Smith. "He was a hick preacher in downtown Los Angeles preaching out of a tent. And nobody even knew who he was or paid attention to him. But for some reason, William Randolph Hearst, the old man, took a liking to him. And he called Mickey and asked him to go to this preacher and give him a helping hand. Hearst had been friendly with Mickey, and I think they helped each other out in different spots.

"So Mickey went down and met Billy Graham. He said he dressed like a hick. He took Graham back to his house and gave him some ties because his ties were kind of loud and garish," laughs Smith. "Graham gave Mickey money to come to Madison Square Garden. And then he gave Mickey more money, which actually he shouldn't have done if he was legitimate. He thought Mickey was going to convert from Judaism to Christianity. Mickey went to the meeting, but he just waved when Billy Graham introduced him. Mickey didn't go down and become converted. Billy Graham didn't like that. Mickey never had any intention of converting.

"From what I understand, Billy Graham was a big phony. He talked about living with your neighbor, yet he lived in a mansion where nobody could get to him. If he was on a plane, he'd buy both seats so no one could sit next to him. Mickey and I knew a guy named Chuck Ashman who at one time was going to write a book about Graham called *Reverend Rip Off*. They stopped him. He wrote a toned-down version, but he couldn't call it *Reverend Rip Off*. Mickey said he was in Billy Graham's counting room once, and there was much more money in Graham's counting room than there was in his own gambling counting room."

Police Chief William H. Parker and the 1957 Mike Wallace Interview

Following Cohen's release from prison in 1956, Los Angeles Police Chief Parker made it his business to catch him at anything he could.

"Chief Parker went out of his way to bother Mickey," said Smith. "He had his men rousting and following Mickey all the time. One time Mickey was at this event on Hollywood Blvd. After the event there were like two hundred people crossing against the light. And Mickey was walking across the light too. They singled Mickey out for a jaywalking ticket. That infuriated him. So he did everything he could do to hurt Parker. And Parker did everything he could do to hurt Mickey."

In 1957 Mike Wallace booked Cohen for his television show, *The Mike Wallace Interview*. Wallace told Cohen to say anything he felt like saying, whatever was on his mind. Lulled into a false sense of security and comfort, the normally outspoken Cohen had even less a filter between his thoughts and what he said.

When asked about killing people, Cohen said, "I have killed no man in the first place that didn't deserve killing by the standards of our way of life…in all these…what you call killings…I had no alternative. It was either my life or their life. You couldn't call those cold-blooded killings."

Regarding Police Chief Parker, Cohen said, "I had a little bit more difficult time than probably somebody else would have because I have a police chief in Los Angeles, California, who happens to be a sadistic degenerate. The man has no decency…a known degenerate, in other words, a sadistic degenerate of the worst type…an alcoholic."

This interview created a media firestorm. Chief Parker sued ABC and Cohen for $2 million.

"Mickey said that he had proof that Parker was an alcoholic. Other people have said that too," said Smith. "A lot of times he would be so drunk that other cops would have to drive him home.

"Mickey said on that *Mike Wallace Interview* that Parker was a sexual degenerate. And they sued ABC, and they settled because they didn't want to go to court. But Mickey had proof that when Parker was in Florida, there were some girls. He tried to have sex with these girls, and he pinched them really bad and made them black and blue. He did some other horrible things and treated them very badly. Mickey knew these girls so he knew what he was talking about. And they probably could have won the suit. Mickey was going to have these girls testify. But ABC didn't want to go through all that. So they had the hatred and animosity until Mickey went to jail the second time. While Mickey was in jail, Parker died."

Political Friends and Adversaries

"Mickey couldn't have operated for ten minutes if he hadn't had the sheriff of Los Angeles on his payroll, the district attorney on his payroll, and all these politicians paid off. He had all these enterprises in Burbank, Pasadena, Hollywood, the black district, and Beverly Hills. He had gambling all over the place. Mickey had casino operations, bookmaker operations, and commissioned bookmaker operations," said Smith.

"That's why it really gets to me that these new books about Mickey say that he was involved with swindling and blackmailing women or that he was involved in prostitution. Brenda Allen was the madam at that time, and the police department and the vice squad were her partners. Mickey didn't need to get involved with this type of thing. At that time his problem was what to do with the money he was making. Not how to get more money. He had too much money as it was and was trying to launder it. He was never involved with prostitution or narcotics, and these writers want to say that he was. But he wasn't."

Allegedly, the sixth floor district attorney's office was on the take. "Mickey often boasted to me that Edmund G. 'Pat' Brown, who was the district attorney and later governor, was his partner."

During the 1970s Cohen and Smith were dining at Chasen's. The current Governor Jerry Brown (the son of Edmund G. "Pat" Brown) was outraged when he saw that Cohen would be dining there. "He was sitting next to our table. But that was Mickey's table because it was close to the door so Mickey could walk in. He was crippled at the time and needed the table by the door," explains Smith. "All of a sudden there is all this confusion. The governor said either they're going to leave, or we're going to leave. And Dave Chasen said, 'I'm not telling Mickey to leave.' So the governor left with his whole party, and we stayed. And you can believe that burned up Jerry Brown—that they would let the governor go before Mickey? They stormed out before they finished their meal. I often wonder if they paid their check; probably not."

Cohen, while publicizing his book, went to the Press Club in San Francisco. Someone at the Press Club told Cohen that Brown had just been there and was talking about Cohen. "What did he say?" asked Cohen. The fellow at the Press Club replied, "He said you were too despicable to mention." Cohen laughed, "His father didn't seem to think so."

In 1962 Governor "Pat" Brown had President John F. Kennedy send an emissary, Richard R. Rogan, to Cohen in prison to get a confidential statement regarding his association with Richard Milhous Nixon. There was a possibility of shortening Cohen's sentence he was told; however, that never came to pass. Brown was preparing for the next gubernatorial campaign where he would be running against Nixon and was looking for ammunition.

Cohen's association with Nixon dated back to the 1940s. "Mickey had an attorney named Murray Chotiner. One day Chotiner wanted to see Mickey about a young guy who was going into politics. This guy was running against Helen Gahagan Douglas, the wife of actor Melvyn Douglas. The young politician was Richard Milhous Nixon from Whittier, California," said Smith. "Mickey didn't know him from anything. So Mickey said it was OK and that he'd help this kid.

"So when they brought in this young guy who looked like some hayseed, Mickey threw a big party for him at the Knickerbocker Hotel, and he invited all the bookmakers and mob guys from the whole area to raise money for Nixon. That party financed his first campaign, and he did beat Helen Gahagan Douglas.

"When Nixon was still president, Mickey asked Murray Chotiner if they would allow a guy named Gyp DeCarlo, who was in prison and dying of cancer, to go to a prison closer to his home so his family could visit him easier. Mickey asked Chotiner, and Chotiner asked Nixon to not only move him but also pardon him. So they let the guy go." Angelo "Gyp" DeCarlo was released from prison in December, 1972, and died on October 20, 1973, five days before a deadline to pay a fine of $20,000.00 from his 1970 conviction.

Cohen recalled the 1959 McClellan hearings in his book and stated that there was no question that Chief William Parker and Bobby Kennedy had everything to do with his being indicted. He also remembered Kennedy's interrogation of him on live television.

"The hearing was supposed to be closed for the day. But the TV was still on and all that bullshit," wrote Cohen. "So Kennedy says, 'Now off the record—you say you're a gentleman and all that. Let me ask you one question, and it has nothing to do with what we're here for, but what's the meaning in the underworld or the racket world when somebody's lights are about to be put out?' So I says, 'Look it, I don't know what you're talking about. I'm not an electrician.' Boy, he got as hot as a pistol. He starts to come down off the podium where he was sitting with all them senators. So McClellan grabbed him by the sleeve, because if he had come down there, I would [have] torn him apart, kicked his fucking head in, and I would have had every reason in the world to do so."

Jim Smith recalled that Bobby Kennedy wanted Cohen to be an informer. "Mickey was convicted and sent to Alcatraz, which [was] also ridiculous because that was supposed to be for convicted murderers. Income tax evasion is a white-collar crime. He should have been sent to some nothing place…some country club jail. So while he was in there, Bobby Kennedy came to see him, and they offered him a deal. If he would rat on Paul 'the waiter' Ricca and Tony 'Joe Batters' Accardo, Kennedy would make a deal with him for maybe a lighter sentence. I don't know what they would have done exactly. But Mickey wouldn't do that. He did every day of his time. He did over eleven years of a fifteen-year sentence. That's been the longest for income tax evasion ever."

Being an informer, a "rat," was something Cohen could never do.

"It wasn't so much to protect those guys…as much as just not being an informer," elaborated Smith. "Mickey said he could never look in the mirror. Anybody who does that, he didn't even know how they could look in the mirror. It's not just protecting the other person…it's a code you've grown up with. And he would feel unfaithful to himself if he violated that code. But he liked Ricca and Accardo anyway. He wouldn't have done that. It wasn't his make-up or his style. So he did every day of his time. And the last nine years he did crippled."

The Rat Pack and Other Hollywood Friends

When Cohen was first released from prison in January 1972, Sammy Davis Jr. was opening at the Coconut Grove. Smith called for reservations, only to be told that there was no way they could accommodate any additional guests. When Smith mentioned the reservation was for Mickey Cohen, the maître d' changed his attitude completely; they pushed tables aside for Cohen and his twelve guests.

"Mickey really liked Frank Sinatra; I didn't share that sentiment with

Mickey Cohen, Jim Smith, and brother Harry Cohen (back wearing hat) on January 7, 1972 when Cohen was released from prison. Most prisoners receive their personal belongings in an envelope upon their release. Cohen's watch, ring, and other belongings were never returned to him—stolen by insiders within the prison. (AP Photo/ William Straeter 1972)

him," said Smith. "He liked the whole clan—Dean Martin and Sammy Davis Jr. Every Thursday night, they had boxing at the Olympic auditorium. We used to take Sammy's father with us when we were in town. He loved boxing so we would do that.

"I liked Dean Martin the most of all of them. Sinatra was a pain in the neck. I always thought he was a *prima donna*. They say he was a tough guy, but he always had two bodyguards with him. The only time he had a problem was with Carl Cohen at the Sands Hotel in Las Vegas. Sinatra was drunk and driving a golf cart around and through the hotel. The security guards didn't want to bother with him so they called Carl Cohen, the casino boss at the Sands at that time. He came down and Sinatra got smart with Carl who finally punched

Sinatra and knocked his caps out. That's when he quit the Sands and went to Caesar's Palace.

"Frank acted like he was a king," recalled Smith who pointed out that Sinatra was never rude to him and actually used to call him Champ. However, he had seen him treat fans and waiters badly. Once Smith even told Cohen, "As far as I'm concerned, Sinatra's a son of a bitch." And Cohen replied, "Jim, you gotta remember, it's OK if a guy is a son of a bitch, as long as he's your son of a bitch. He's all right with you, isn't he? Don't worry about anyone else."

"Dean Martin, if you met him, acted like the guy next door. You'd think he was a plumber or something. He didn't act like a big celebrity. But Frank, he wanted you to think he was a king. That was just the difference in their personalities. Sammy Davis Jr. was all right. I saw him shortly before he died. He shook hands with me and introduced me to some guy he was with and said, 'Jim's my friend from the old days.' And then about one week later he was dead. I really liked Sammy's father; he was a great guy."

Cohen and Jim Smith used to enjoy going to Chasen's restaurant. The owner, Dave Chasen, was an old friend of Cohen's. They met when Chasen was running a little chili stand.

"Dave Chasen was a wonderful guy. He always came over to say hello to Mickey. Dave would sit with us sometimes, but his wife Maude would never come over or even say hello," recollected Smith. "As a matter of fact, we used to go to about twenty restaurants at that time in the 1970s. Dave Chasen was the only owner who came over to us. He took me aside one time and said, 'Jim, I want to tell you something. After you guys leave, the FBI comes over and Photostats the check.' I thanked him for telling us.

"The FBI used to try to trap Mickey to see if he spent more than what he declared that he made. Out of all the restaurants we went to, Dave Chasen was the only one who ever told us what was going on. He went out on a limb to let us know.

"We enjoyed going to Chasen's on Thursday nights because every major actor went there that night because it was the help's night off. These guys didn't want to stay home," said Smith. "At one table there would be James Stewart sitting with Alfred Hitchcock. Or there would be Gregory Peck,

Kirk Douglas, Burt Lancaster, or any number of top celebrities. We took Redd Foxx, who was a good friend of Mickey's, to Chasen's for the first time; he'd never been there and wanted to try their chili.

"Mickey always sat at the same table and never went to anybody's table. If people didn't want to see him or didn't want to know about him, he didn't want to be around them. But every time we went to Chasen's, there were always many celebrities who came over to see Mickey and thank him for past favors or just say hello. We'd see Ernest Borgnine, Phil Silvers, Red Buttons, Robert Ryan, Danny Thomas, and Robert Wagner. George Burns would always come by because he knew Neddie Herbert, one of Mickey's men who was shot during the war of the Sunset Strip.

"One time Danny Thomas came up to see Mickey. Danny would say, 'If anyone messes with me they will meet their maker.' And he pulls back his coat, and he had a gun in a little holster on the side of his coat, which we thought was kind of stupid. But maybe he needed protection, who knows?

"I'll tell you a funny thing about Robert Wagner," continued Smith. "Every Thursday night he'd come over and say hello to Mickey. When Robert Wagner would walk back to his table, he'd always ask me, 'Jim, who was that guy again?' And I'd have to explain. Mickey had been in prison for eleven years, and that's when Wagner made *It Takes a Thief.* Before that he was a young guy making movies. But Mickey never did know who Robert Wagner was."

Mickey's Women

Mickey Cohen married just once to Lavonne Weaver, a dance instructor who knew how to fly a plane, which intrigued him. They married in the middle of the night, and Cohen had his dog Tuffy there. The preacher insisted the dog leave. There was an argument, and then finally the preacher said Tuffy could stay, and they got married.

The couple stayed together for fifteen years, When Cohen returned from McNeil Island, they divorced. In Cohen's autobiography he gallantly said she was at no fault whatsoever.

The day that her divorce was final, Lavonne eloped with Sam Farkas, a former bodyguard of Cohen's. At the time of their marriage, Farkas claimed he had reformed and was in the steel business.

"Mickey didn't like that they did that, but he stayed friendly with his wife. But he was never friendly with Sam Farkas. He was a big, kind of stupid guy. He ended up being a bookmaker. He was OK. Mickey wasn't going to bother him, but Sam didn't know that," laughs Smith. "So Sam was always a bit leery about that. He sort of, at that time, took his life in his own hands. But Mickey would never have done anything about that."

Following, and even before, his divorce from Lavonne, Cohen liked to keep company with strippers and starlets.

"They were all kind of hustling girls," explains Smith. "None of them were pillars of virtue. They were rounders and pretty much the same type of girls. There was a girl named Arlene Stevens and a stripper named Beverly Hills. I didn't think much of Sandy Hagen or stripper Liz Renay. Mickey had plenty of girls, but they were strippers, hustlers, nightclub girls, good-time girls, party girls. He liked showy blondes that were sort of ostentatious. He liked short women because he himself was short.

"None of these women held a candle to stripper Candy Barr, though. In my opinion, she was the ultimate of all those women. She was also very comical and fun to be around," Smith recalled. "One day when I was first out here in California, Mickey came down to the gym and was watching me train. He said, 'What are you doing tonight?' And I said, 'Nothing special.' And he says, 'Why don't you meet me at the Largo later tonight, and we'll have dinner.'"

The Largo was a club on Sunset Boulevard where Candy Barr appeared. "That night I

Exotic dancer Candy Barr and Mickey Cohen in 1959. (AP Photo/The Herald Express)

went up to meet him, and I started to go in the door; there was a big doorman there. He says, 'Are you twenty-one?' I said, 'No I'm eighteen.' He says, 'Well you can't come in then. You've got to be twenty-one to get in here.' I said, 'Oh, OK, I'm sorry.' I thought about it, and I said, 'Could you tell Mr. Cohen I was here to see him, but I couldn't get in.' And he thought about it and said, 'Which Cohen is that?' I said, 'Mickey Cohen; I was supposed to meet him here.' He says, 'Well, why didn't you say so?' He grabbed me by the hand and took me over to Mickey's table, and he said, 'Mickey! Mickey! Your friend is here' And he forgot that I wasn't twenty-one and offered me a drink and couldn't do enough for me. I didn't tell Mickey he wouldn't let me in. So we sat down and watched the show and everything was fine.

"Mickey cared quite a bit for Lita Baron (ex-wife of Rory Calhoun) in the 1970s. The women kind of came and went. He liked them and was generous with money. Not that he gave them money. But they liked the lifestyle…going to Chasen's and meeting actors. We went to a lot of fights and plays that Mickey slept through," laughs Smith. "The women liked being out at all the top spots. It was pretty interesting for them.

"One time we went out of town and took this woman with us. We had rooms with an adjoining door. It was the first time this woman had ever traveled with us," explains Smith.

"Mickey used to carry several thousand dollars with him, especially when we were out of town. So he would always ask me when he went into the shower to hold his bankroll, just in case something happened or someone came in. Mickey had a cleanliness compulsion and would shower for two or three hours. This time I noticed that he didn't ask me to hold his money.

"I was just relaxing in my room when all of a sudden, this woman rushes into my room. 'Oh my God, Jim, something terrible has happened!' I laughed and asked what terrible thing happened. She says, 'Someone broke into our room while Mickey was in the shower.' I asked, 'What do you mean someone broke into your room? Where were you, what were you doing?' She said, 'I was asleep.' I said, 'Oh, you were asleep?' Then she said that somebody had stolen *part of* Mickey's money. I laughed—part of his money? How could they steal part of his money? She said Mickey gave her the money to hold, that she laid it on the table, and somebody broke in. I said, 'If they broke in, why wouldn't they have taken the whole thing?' She said she didn't know. But she said, 'You've got to do one thing for me.' And I asked her what. And she said, 'Mickey made me promise that I wouldn't tell you.'

"Mickey didn't want me to know that she robbed him," laughed Smith. "He was embarrassed. But I didn't say anything to him. All three of us were getting ready to go to dinner, and he was just sitting there. He's all sad-faced and in a sour, bad mood. She finally went to the bathroom or someplace. And I said, 'Jesus Christ, Mickey, so you got robbed? So she robbed you? What's the big deal? You're a sucker anyway.' 'Jesus Christ,' he said, she *had* to tell you. It was bad enough that she robbed me.' I asked how much she took. And he said $1,500.00. She counted out $1,500.00, and she thought he had five or six thousand, and he wouldn't know the difference. He knew every quarter. She didn't know that he counted himself down before he handed her the money.

"I asked him why he handed it to her in the first place, and he said that he wanted to see if she could pass the test. I said that she failed the test. 'Why did she have to rob me?' he asked. I said, 'She thinks you're a sucker, that's why.' And after that Mickey was OK. He didn't want me to know, but he gave himself up."

Cohen's cleanliness compulsion actually saved his life. Cohen was in the bathroom washing his hands when the gunmen rushed into his haberdashery and killed Hooky Rothman. Cohen's constant washing of his hands and several hour-long showers would today be diagnosed as Obsessive-Compulsive Disorder. The prison psychiatrists told him that he was either trying to cleanse his soul of evil deeds or wash the newsprint from his hands. When Cohen was a little boy, he sold newspapers and was constantly washing the ink off. Cohen related to Smith that he was worried where a person's hands might have been before they shook hands with him.

"I remember that after he took his two-hour showers, he would come out and put a hat on his head and throw baby powder all over himself. He put the hat on so he wouldn't get powder in his hair. He didn't have much hair, but he didn't want powder in it. Sometimes I'd come in when he was dressing, into this whole cloud of smoke. I'd ask, 'Mick, are you in there?'" laughs Smith. "He used up all the hot water in his entire apartment building with those long showers. So Mickey had to have his own water heater put on the roof, otherwise no one else could have taken a warm shower."

Smith was with Cohen during the last attempt on his life. "Mickey didn't like to come home too early. So we always came home around about two o'clock in the morning, sometimes later. This one particular night, we drove into the subterranean garage in his apartment building. We pulled in there, and the elevator was close by. It was a small little elevator that would take us up to the third floor where his apartment was.

"And just as we were going in the elevator, a guy pushed in behind us, and everything happened so fast. The guy shoved in behind us, and all he got to say was 'OK, Mickey.' And he had a gun in his hand. Before he had a chance to do anything, I grabbed him and knocked him down. I was wrestling around with him a little bit. And just to show you how Mickey was…there was a rail in the elevator. Mickey couldn't walk too well because he was crippled. He walked with a cane. Yet he was holding onto the rail kicking this guy in the head. I said, 'We don't need you to keep doing that. I've got it under control.' Freddy Sica came over a little while later and took the guy away. I don't know what happened after that."

Smith said that even though Cohen was partially paralyzed, he still liked to try to keep in shape by sparring with him. "I'd put Mickey up against the wall and we'd spar. Once in a while, he'd get a good punch in and he'd clap and laugh; he really loved it when he could get me."

Corrections of Misconceptions

Jim Smith says that most of the books and films that depict Cohen are, for the most part, fiction.

"In the last few years, there have been three or four books written about Mickey. And every one of them has maybe 10 percent truth to them. Everything has been fictionalized and fantasized," complains Smith. "These authors, who know nothing, go to police files or FBI files or newspaper clippings, and they take a little bit out of that. What I've also noticed is that new authors will take from the author who wrote the first book, which was no good in the first place. Sometimes they get a shred of truth, but they don't know what the story really was, so they make their own story.

"There are several stories that recent books about Mickey bring up. One is about Howard Chappell. He was a cop who inferred that Mickey was dealing in narcotics. When he heard that, Mickey, who was furious, ran down to his office and got into a big fight with him. This guy is 6"5" and Mickey is like 5"5", and there were three or four other guys there. So there was a big fight. The story was told in a book recently, and they had it completely wrong.

"Another story that was recently butchered was about the Villa Capri. The writer said that Mickey beat up a waiter. Mickey wouldn't do that. He always bent over backward to be nice to waiters. The story didn't mention that Sammy Davis Jr.'s father, who was with us, had recently had a heart attack. The waiter kept bumping him. Mickey says, 'What's the matter with you? Why do you keep bumping this old man?' And the waiter got smart with Mickey, and he hit him. The book was making out like Mickey was picking on some waiter. He never did that; he was defending Sammy Davis Jr.'s father.

"The next thing they tried to say was that in the 1970s, Mickey was a hidden owner of Gatsby's restaurant. He wasn't a hidden owner at all. They said he had bookmaking and a gambling casino in there. If Gatsby's owners saw that, they must have had a heart attack.

"They've also said that Mickey didn't really like women," said Smith incredulously. "Mickey had tons of women; even in the 1970s when he was already in his sixties and dying of cancer, he still had a woman with him."

According to Jim Smith, films have also missed the mark when portraying Cohen. "The movie *Bugsy* (1991) that Warren Beatty did about Ben Siegel was ridiculous. All he did was play Warren Beatty and use Ben Siegel's name. Harvey Keitel, who played Mickey, is a good actor. But they had one scene where Harvey Keitel as Mickey had a drink in one hand and a cigar in the other. Mickey never smoked or drank. And the scene where Siegel gets hit, they have him wandering around the living room instead of sitting on the couch. Warren Beatty made a movie, but he didn't do a movie on Ben Siegel. He just used the name. *The Gangster Squad* (2012), starring Sean Penn, is also complete fiction. Again, they just used Mickey's name. Mob movies are never accurate. Tony Danza once said to me, 'The people in Iowa don't know the difference, Jim.'"

Smith was also friends with Tony "the ant" Spilotro, who was portrayed by Joe Pesci in *Casino* (1995). "Tony Spilotro, in my estimation, it seems everybody wants to portray him as a loud and sadistic killer. I was around him on many, many occasions in Las Vegas, Los Angeles, and Chicago. I always found him to be a gentleman; he was on the quiet side and was always very nice. No matter what time he got home, whether it was two o'clock in the morning or four o'clock in the morning, he'd always get up the next morning and fix breakfast for his son. He thought it was important to spend quality time with his little boy. The way Pesci played him in *Casino* was ridiculous. He had him acting like an animal. I asked Nicholas Pileggi about this one time because he wrote the script. I asked why he made him like a wild man. And Pileggi said that's the way Pesci wanted to play him. And he let it go at that. Spilotro wasn't like that at all."

The Real Mickey Cohen—Friends, Humor, and Heart

"When Mickey first came home from prison in 1972, he received a phone call from Jo Wyatt who worked in one of the Las Vegas casinos. There was a girl who worked there who was a shill. That's somebody who acts like they are gambling, but they are really working for the house, gambling with the house's money, and attracting people to the table," explains Smith. "Anyway, this girl had a five-year-old daughter who needed hospitalization really bad. Las Vegas didn't have a children's hospital at that time. The little girl needed treatment right away, and the only place she could go was Los Angeles, which had a children's hospital. They called and couldn't get her in. There was no way to get the little girl down there, and her mother didn't have money.

"Now Mickey had been in prison for eleven years, and he didn't have a lot of connections. He called Agnes Underwood, who was a very important woman at the *Herald Examiner* newspaper. She was able to get the girl into the children's hospital, but no one knew how to get her here from Las Vegas. Mickey chartered a helicopter, sent it to Vegas, picked up this little girl, her mother, and Jo Wyatt, and brought them down to Los Angeles.

"They saved the little girl's life, and she was there for a couple of months. And here's Mickey, who is supposed to be this cold-blooded gangster, going to the children's hospital two or three times a week. He's taking her teddy bears and all kinds of stuffed animals. Not only that, he had every mobster in town going too. One day Jimmy Fratianno would bring flowers. The next day Joe Sica would be there with some stuffed animals. After that Freddy Sica would come. And then Frank "Bomp" Bompensiero would show up. There were about ten mobsters in all coming in to see this little girl. She was the most popular girl in that hospital. And Mickey saved her life. He paid the whole tab, which was several thousand dollars even in those days. So this doesn't sound exactly like a cold-blooded killer who didn't care about anyone but himself."

During the early 1950s, when Frank Sinatra was in his slump—not able to sing and not getting any movie roles, Mickey Cohen threw him a testimonial dinner. People brought money. Cohen also gave Sinatra a Cadillac to drive and flew his parents in from New Jersey.

Cohen somehow found out that one of his former reform schools was in trouble. It was near Christmas time and the head of the school asked Cohen if he could help put on a show.

"Mickey got a hold of Redd Foxx, Sammy Davis Jr., Sarah Vaughn, and Gail Fisher. They all performed for free and donated everything," recalled Smith. "Sarah Vaughan brought her own musicians. Mickey wanted to pay them, but she wouldn't let him. Now Mickey didn't make any money out of this; he just put on a great show out of the kindness of his heart."

In addition to his bulldog Tuffy, Cohen also later had a little English bulldog called Mickey Jr. The dog lived the same life that Cohen did. He had a bed made identical to Cohen's bed and a monogrammed bedspread that said MC Jr. and Cohen's bedspread read MC.

"Mickey loved this dog. He would come home at three or four o'clock in the morning and would let the dog out for a little bit," said Smith. "One night the dog ran out into traffic and got hit by a car. Now he wasn't

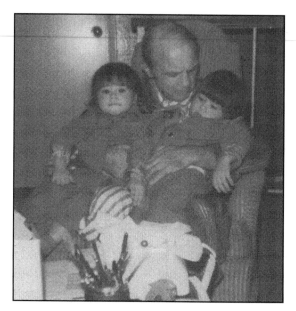

Mickey Cohen cuddling Jim Smith's children, daughter Tina and son Jimmy. (Courtesy of Jim Smith)

dead right away, but he was bleeding badly. Mickey was wearing a beige suit; he picked the dog up in his arms, and the dog is bleeding all over his suit. Mickey put him in his car and drove to a real doctor, not a veterinarian. They went to the hospital and did everything they could to save little Mickey Jr's life. But they couldn't save him.

"Mickey had people that he loved," said Smith. "I have two children, a girl, Tina, and a boy, Jimmy. He *loved* those kids. They used to call him "Uncle Mickey." He let them sit in his lap, and he would play, talk, and kid with them." It seems that Mickey, who never had any children, thought of Smith and his wife and children as a surrogate family.

"Mickey would never have anything to do with narcotics. As a matter of fact, one time Mickey and I were at a party. And he asks, 'What's that strange smell?' I said, 'Marijuana.' Mickey said, 'That's what it smells like?' I said, 'Yeah.' And he thinks about a minute and yells, '*How* do you know?' " Sounds like a little fatherly concern.

Jim Smith related a funny story about an afternoon spent at the swimming pool in Cohen's apartment complex. Cohen and Smith used to sit at the opposite end from the other tenants. Cohen used to wonder whether the neighbors were discussing him.

"One day this little boy who was about six years old is swimming around. And he swims over to us. And he looked up and yelled 'Hey!' and Mickey asks, 'What?' And the little kid looks at us and asks, 'Are you guys gangsters?' And Mickey says, 'I'm not but he is,' and points at me," laughs Smith. By this time the parents are screaming for the kid to come back. Mickey was always jovial and in a good mood."

Smith recalled enjoyable dinners with Cohen where he exhibited his great sense of humor. "Mickey was always telling jokes. For example, Mickey had sixty-eight professional fights, and so people would talk to him about boxing. Well, very few people knew that I was also a professional fighter at one time. Mickey would stop them from talking, and he would say, 'You know, Jim was a great fighter.' And they would say, 'Really?' I would never say anything about myself or about the fact that I

This was Mickey Cohen's favorite picture of Jim Smith's son Jimmy holding a toy machine gun. He had it framed in his house and would show guests who came over, especially mobsters who would laugh and say, "You're bringing that kid along right." (Courtesy of Jim Smith)

was fighting. I just let Mickey talk because no one wanted to hear what I had to say. And he would say, 'I don't think you know it, but Jim was a welterweight champion.' And they'd say, 'He was a welterweight champion?' And he'd say, 'Yeah, a welterweight champion of the underworld.'

Many times Cohen would take fifteen or so guests to dinner. They would sit at opposite ends of a long table and Cohen would signal Smith if he needed him. They didn't sit together because Smith saw Cohen every day, and the guests naturally wanted a chance to talk to Cohen.

Jim Smith, his wife Myra Smith, Jo Wyatt, and Mickey Cohen.
(Courtesy of Jim Smith)

"My wife Myra went with us occasionally. She didn't go very often because we had kids and she was busy," recalls Smith. "But Mickey would yell down, and he would say, 'Myra, Myra,' until he got her attention. And she'd say, 'Yeah, Mickey.' And he'd say, 'I want to ask you a very important question.' And everybody would get really quiet, and they would be listening. And she'd say, 'Yeah, Mickey, what is it?' And he'd say, 'Tell the truth now.' And she'd say, 'OK.' And he'd ask, 'Did Jim ever have a job?' And she'd yell back, 'Mickey, Jim never worked a day in his life.' And Mickey would clap his hands while laughing, and the whole table would bust up with laughter."

Following Cohen's release from prison, he went to the head neurosurgeon at UCLA, Dr. Rubenstein, because of the paralysis he suffered due to the near fatal beating he received in the federal penitentiary. Dr. Rubenstein happened to mention that he was having a very important wedding anniversary, and that he was just taking his wife to a neighborhood restaurant. Cohen asked the doctor where he'd like to go. The doctor said Scandia, but he had no hope of getting in because it was the top restaurant in town among celebrities, and there was a six-week waiting list. Cohen asked how many people he'd like to bring, and Dr. Rubenstein answered four. Cohen smiled at Jim Smith and asked him to call the restaurant. "I called and asked Leonard, the maître d', to please give Dr. Rubenstein Mickey's table and to hold the bill," explained Smith. "The doctor couldn't believe it; he was amazed."

Underworld figure Jimmy Fratianno was a good friend of both Smith and Cohen. "Mickey brought Fratianno out in the late 1930s to be a part of his crew. He rose through the ranks to become the west coast executioner," explained Smith. "And you'd never know it because he was friendly, had a good personality, and a great sense of humor. I liked him very much."

One night during the 1970s, Fratianno called Cohen's home, and the answering service rang him through to Smith and Cohen at a restaurant.

"I picked up the phone and it was Jimmy Fratianno," remembered Smith. "Fratianno said, 'I have a big problem.' And I asked, 'What's the problem?' And he says, 'I got married today, and my wife knows I'm an important guy.' I kidded him, 'Everybody knows you're an important guy. So what's the problem?' And he said, 'My wife's dream is to go to the Scandia restaurant. And we're here.' And I asked again, 'What's the problem?' And he said, 'The problem is we can't get into this goddamned place.' I said, 'What do you mean you can't get it in? You just told me you were in.' He says, 'No, these guys…these suckers…they don't know who I am. They've never heard of me. They won't let me in.'

"So I kidded with him again and said, 'Jim, here's what you got to do. You put your name down on the list. In six weeks you come back and you can get in,'" laughed Smith. Fratianno says, 'Oh come on. This is very important. I'm going to look like a bum if we don't get in here.' I told him to look around for a guy named Leonard, and finally he came to the phone. I said, 'Leonard, Mr. Fratianno is a friend of ours. Give him Mickey's booth and save the bill for us.' Fratianno came back on the phone and thanked us. He claimed we made a hero out of him to his wife and said, 'Thanks, Jim. I figured a joint like this, you guys would be juiced in pretty good.'

"Fratianno had a reputation as the executioner," recalled Smith. "One time I was riding with Frank "Bomp" Bompensiero (head of the mafia in San Diego), and he mentioned that he had noticed that I was pretty friendly with Fratianno. And I said that we got along well together.

Bompensiero warned me to be careful of Fratianno. He said that a lot of people thought they were friendly with him, and they wound up dead. And I said I'd watch my step. The funny thing is that Bompensiero was warning me about Fratianno, and about one year later Fratianno helped kill Bompensiero."

Two of Cohen's closest friends were underworld figures Joe and Freddy Sica. They were associates for many years. There were actually seven Sica brothers; however, Joe and Freddy achieved the most notoriety.

"Freddy Sica was an excellent cook. A lot of guys would come over, and he'd cook for everybody. And one time I walked into the kitchen to get a drink of water, and Freddy asked me to please leave. He said, 'I can't concentrate with people in here.' So I said, 'I'm sorry Freddy, I just wanted a drink,'" laughs Smith. "He thought I was going to tell him how to cook. Like I know anything about cooking. Freddy considered it an art. He did not want to be bothered while he was cooking Italian food."

One of the big events of the 1970s in the underworld was the wedding of mob boss Frank Bompensiero's granddaughter.

Joe Stadino, Frank "Bomp" Bompensiero, Chris Petti, Joe Pietro, Jim Smith, Mickey Cohen, Marie Bompensiero, and Fred Sica (Courtesy of Jim Smith)

"All kinds of both mob people and legitimate people were invited to the wedding. It was a really big affair in San Diego," remembers Smith. "Mickey was on parole, and he had to ask permission to leave Los Angeles County, and they granted him permission to go.

"Well, Joe Sica was also one of Mickey's associates going back to Ben Siegel. Joe had just finished up a fourteen-year sentence at Leavenworth. All the mob guys were going: Chris Petti, Tony Spilotro, Mickey, and Joe's brother Freddy.

"Joe went to his parole officer and asked permission and was denied because he was not allowed to associate with known hoodlums. So Joe comes to the apartment one day, and he's telling Mickey, 'I don't understand how you can go, and I can't go.' And Mickey says, 'Jesus Christ, it's very obvious. They don't want hoodlums. They know you're a hoodlum, and you're not allowed to go. It's very understandable to me,'" Smith laughed.

The adorable Smith children, Tina and Jimmy, with notorious underworld figure Joe Sica. (Courtesy of Jim Smith)

"One of the things Mickey and I enjoyed the most was ribbing each other. One day we were in San Francisco, and I asked Mickey what he wanted to do that afternoon. He said whatever I wanted to do. I said I had heard that they were giving tours of Alcatraz. And Mickey said, 'No! Goddamn it! I've already toured that damn place! Why don't you go? I'll wait here.' Smith laughed, "Needless to say, I didn't take the tour that day. I was just giving Mickey a bad time."

Smith did take the tour of Alcatraz years after Mickey's death. He saw a picture on the wall of the cell house of a man wearing a hat identified as Cohen. "That picture was not of Mickey Cohen, it was of Frank Carbo. I told the tour guide who was dressed as a guard, and he didn't believe me. But that picture wasn't of Mickey. He asked me how I knew, but I wasn't going to tell him. There are only eight thousand pictures of Mickey out there, and they had the wrong picture up there. For all I know, it's still up there."

Cohen sued the federal government in 1966 for failing to protect him in prison when he was attacked by Berl Estes McDonald. This attack left Cohen disabled for the remainder of his life. His attorney was Melvin Belli. Cohen won the case and was awarded $110,000.00, which could not be attached for his tax lien. It was to be used for physical rehabilitation and medical purposes. Neither Cohen nor his attorney Belli, who was entitled to legal fees, ever received the judgment.

Smith discussed Cohen's relationship with authors and the press. "He didn't want people to give him the worst of it, and he didn't want them to give him the best of it. He didn't mind how they portrayed him but just asked that they be fair. They wouldn't do that. A lot of writers came to write stories about him, and he would accommodate them. He asked them to send a copy of the story, and they never would send an advance copy. And they always went on to portray him as a sadistic killer because that is what sells. Any of the things I've just told you they don't put in."

With all the attempts on his life from gunfire to bombings, it was cancer that finally took his life. On July 29, 1976, Cohen passed away peacefully at the age of sixty-two.

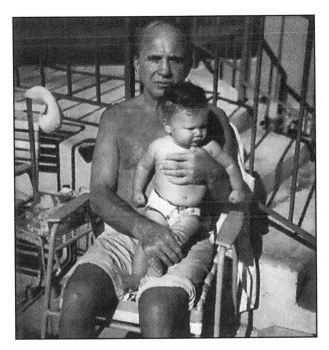

Mickey Cohen holding little Jimmy Smith.
(Courtesy of Jim Smith).

"Nobody ever really knew what Mickey was like," said Smith. "What was he like inside? What did he feel? What was his philosophy of life? How was he as a human being?"

Somewhere there is a woman who as a little girl had her life saved by a whole team of individuals. However, one man in particular spurred this process on. Without this man, she wouldn't be here. He didn't just pay for whatever needed to be done and walk away. He made sure that little girl was happy, had a lot of visitors, and felt loved while she was hospitalized in a strange city. She must have memories of an entertaining, sweet bear of a man who came to visit her in the hospital. That man was Mickey Cohen.

Bibliography

Recommended Reading, Websites & Documentaries

Books and Periodicals

Anger, Kenneth. *Hollywood Babylon*. San Francisco, CA: Straight Arrow Books, 1981.

Austin, John. *Hollywood's Unsolved Mysteries*. New York, NY: Shapolsky Publishers, 1990.

Bennett Joan, and Lois Kibbee. *The Bennett Playbill*. New York: Holt, Winehart & Winston, 1st ed., 1970.

Bernstein, Matthew. *Walter Wanger: Hollywood Independent*. Berkeley and Los Angeles, CA: University of California Press, 1st ed., 1994.

Blake, Robert. *Tales of a Rascal*. Black Rainbow Publications, 2011.

Bray, Christopher. *Sean Connery: A Biography*. New York: Pegasus, 2011.

Buckley, Michael. "Gig Young: Were Life Simpler than It Is He'd Have Fared Better," *Films in Review*, February 1971.

Chapling, Lita Grey and Morton Cooper. My Life with Charlie Chaplin. Brattleboro, Vermont: Bernard Greis Associates, 1966.

Cohen Mickey, and John Peer Nugent. *Mickey Cohen: In My Own Words* as told to John Peer Nugent, Englewood Cliffs, New Jersey: Prentice Hall International, Inc., 1975.

Crane, Cheryl. *Detour: A Hollywood Story*. New York: Arbor House-Morrow , 1988.

Davies, Marion. *The Times We Had: Life with William Randolph Hearst.* New York: Ballantine Books, 1st ed., (March 12, 1985).

Donati, William. *The Life and Death of Thelma Todd*. Jefferson, North Carolina: McFarland Publishers, 2012.

Dryan, Martin, and John Blosser. *The National Examiner*. American Media, Inc., August 27, 2012.

Edmonds, Andy. *Hot Toddy: The True Story of Hollywood's Most Sensational Murder.* New York: William Morrow & Company, 1st ed., 1989.

Eells, George. *Final Gig, The Man Behind the Murder*. Orlando, FL: Harcourt, 1st ed., 1991.

Englert, Rod, and Kathy Passero. *Blood Secrets: Chronicles of a Crime Scene Reconstructionist*. New York: Thomas Dunne Books, 2010.

Finstad, Suzanne. *Natasha: The Biography of Natalie Wood*. New York, NY: Harmony Books, 2001.

Fleming, E. J.. *The Fixers*. Jefferson, NC: McFarland Publishers, 2004.

———. *The Life and Famous Death of the MGM Director and Husband of Harlow*. Jefferson, NC: McFarland Publishers, 2009.

Giroux, Robert. *A Deed of Death*. New York: Knopf, 1st ed., 1990.

Goffard, Christopher, Kate Mather and Richard Winton, "New Twist in Wood's Death", *Los Angeles Times*, January 15, 2013

Golden, Eve. *Platinum Girl: The Life and Legends of Jean Harlow*. New York: Abbeville Press, 1991.

Graysmith, Robert. *The Murder of Bob Crane*. New York, NY: Crown, 1993.

Gosch, Martin A., and Richard Hammer. New York: Little Brown and Company, 1975. *The Last Testament of Lucky Luciano*.

Grobel, Lawrence. Christopher Walken Interview, *Playboy Magazine*. Sage Publications, Inc. September 1997.

Hearst, Patricia, and Corneila Frances Bidle. *Murder at San Simeon*, New York: Pocket, 1st ed., 1997.

Henderson, Jan Allan. *Speeding Bullet: The Life and Bizarre Death of Superman*. Publisher: Michael Bifulco, 2007.

Higham, Charles. *Murder in Hollywood, Solving a Silent Screen Mystery*. Madison, WI: University of Wisconsin Press, 2006.

Kashner, Sam. *Hollywood Kryptonite: The Bulldog, The Lady, and the Death of Superman*. New York: St. Martin's Press, 1st ed., 1996.

Kellow, Brian. *The Bennetts: An Acting Family*. Lexington, KY: The University Press of Kentucky, 1st ed., 2004.

King, Gary C.. *Murder In Hollywood: The Secret Life and Mysterious Death of Bonny Lee Bakley*. New York: St. Martin's Paperbacks, 2001.

Kirkpatrick, Sidney D. *Cast of Killers*. NY: 186 Dutton, NY, 1st ed., 1986.

Lambert, Gavin. *Natalie Wood*, New York: Alfred A. Knopf, 2004.

Leigh, Janet, There Really Was a Hollywood, New York: Doubleday, 1984.

Lewis, Brad. *Hollywood's Celebrity Gangster, The Incredible Life and Times of Mickey Cohen*. New York: Enigma Books, 2007.

Lewis, Monica., with Dean Lamanna. *Hollywood Through My Eyes: The Life and Loves of a Golden Age Siren*, 1st ed. Brule, WI: Cable Publishing, 2011.

Lisa, Sophie, Jewel, Tatiana, and Jennifer, as told to Joanne Parrent with Bruce W. Cook. Los Angeles, CA: Dove Books. *Once More with Feeling—You'll Never Make Love in this Town Again*. 1996.

Long, Bruce. *William Desmond Taylor: A Dossier*. Metuchen, NJ: Scarecrow Press, 2004.

Loy, Myrna, and James Kotsilibas-Daviies. *Being and Becoming*. New York: Donald I. Fine, Inc., 1988.

Marx, Samuel. *Deadly Illusions: Jean Harlow and the Murder of Paul Bern*. New York: Random House 1st ed., 1990.

McDougal, Dennis and Mary Murphy. *Blood Cold: Fame Sex and Murder in Hollywood*, New York: Onyx, 2002.

Merrill, Gary. *Bette, Rita, and the Rest of My Life*. New York: Berkley, 1990.

Milton, Joyce. Tramp: The Life of Charlie Chaplin. Los Angeles: Premier Digital Publishing, 1996.

Morella, Joe, and Edward Z. Epstein. *Gable, Lombard, Powell, and Harlow.* New York: Dell, 1975.

Munn, Michael. *The Hollywood Murder Casebook.* United Kingdom: Headline Book Publishing Limited, 1988.

New York Times News Service, Joan Bennett Obituary, *New York Times,* December 9, 1990

Noyes, Pete. *The Real L. A. Confidential.* Create-A-Space Publishing Platform, 2010.

Otash, Fred, and Raymond Strait. "The Whole Truth" (Unpublished).

Root, Eric, Dale Crawford, and Raymond Strait. *My Private Diary of My Life with Lana*, Beverly Hills, CA: Dove Books, 1996.

Rulli, Marti, and Dennis Davern. *Goodbye Natalie, Goodbye Splendour.* New York: E-Rights/E-Reads Ltd. Publishers, 2009

Russell, Rosalind. *Life is a Banquet.* New York: Random House, Inc., 1st ed., 1977.

Shulman, Irving. *Harlow: An Intimate Biography.* New York: Random House, 1964.

Stenn, David. *Bombshell: The Life of Jean Harlow.* New York: Doubleday, 1st ed., 1993.

Taves, Brian. *Thomas Ince: Hollywood's Independent Pioneer.* Lexington, KY: University of Kentucky, 2011.

Turner, Lana. *The Lady, The Legend, The Truth*. New York: Dutton, 1983.

Wagner, Robert. *Pieces of My Heart*. New York: IT Books Reprint Edition, 2009.

Wellman, W. F. Bill. *It's Made to Sell—Not to Drink*. Bloomington, IN: AuthorHouse, 1st ed., 2006.

Young, Elaine. *A Million Dollars Down*. New York: Dell, 1979.

Internet

Angelo DeCarlo; http://en.wikipedia.org/wiki/Angelo_DeCarlo

Bob Crane 1971 Interview; http://m.youtube.com/watch?v=ohFWIbovqw8

Bob Crane, Former WICC Host, Up for Radio Hall of Fame, Julie Burgeson; http://www.stamfordadvocate.com/news/article/Bob-Crane-former-WICC-host-up-for-Radio-Hall-of-2670233.php

Vote for Bob Crane, July 2011; http://vote4bobcrane.blogspot.com/2011_07_01_archive.html

Bugsy Siegel; http://en.wikipedia.org/wiki/Bugsy_Siegel

Edelman, Diane, "The Daughter of Las Vegas: an interview with Millicent Siegel" http://www.dtravelsround.com/2012/07/25/daughter-las-vegas-interview-millicent-siegel/

Lana Wood, Captain Says Wagner Left Wood To Teach Her a Lesson; http://www.tmz.com/2011/11/18/natalie-wood-sister-lana-wood-robert-wagner-video-homicide-investigation/

Kulzer, Dina-Marie, Portrait of Harlow: The Original Blonde Bombshell
http://www.classichollywoodbios.com/jeanharlow.htm

Kulzer, Dina-Marie, Natalie Wood: A Tribute
http://www.classichollywoodbios.com/nataliewood.htm

Rosenbaum, Joseph, Hollywood Confidential
http://www.chicagoreader.com/chicago/hollywoodconfidential/
Content?oid=908386

Avrech, Robert J., Joan Bennett Wants You to be Attractive
http://www.seraphicpress.com/joan-bennett-wants-you-to-be-attractive/

Television and DVD

20/20, "Bob Crane," ABC Television Network, 2006

48 Hours, "Vanity Fair: Hollywood Scandal," November 19, 2011

Biography, "Bob Crane—Double Life," A & E Television Network, February 8, 2000

Biography, "George Reeves: The Perils of a Superhero", February 9, 2000

Biography, "Jean Harlow," A & E Television Network, May 20, 1996

Biography, "Natalie Wood: Child of Hollywood," A & E Television Network, 2003

"*Captured on Film: The True Story of Marion Davies*," Turner Classic Movies, 2001

City Confidential, "Old Hollywood, Deadly Secrets," A & E Television Network, January 6, 2007

Dr. Phil, "Robert Blake: The Man behind the Murder Headlines," Syndicated, September 20, 2012

E! Mysteries and Scandals, "Jean Harlow," "E" Entertainment Television Network, May 11, 1998

E! Mysteries and Scandals, "William Randolph Hearst," "E" Entertainment Television Network, August 10, 1998

E! Mysteries and Scandals, "Thelma Todd," "E" Entertainment Television Network, April 20, 1998

E! True Hollywood Story, "Bob Crane," "E" Entertainment Television Network, January 26, 1999

E! True Hollywood Story, "Natalie Wood," "E" Entertainment Television Network, December 14, 1997

E! True Hollywood Story, "Robert Blake," "E" Entertainment Television Network, April 28, 2002

Extra, "Edward Lozzi," Syndicated, 1999

Inside Edition, "George Reeves Segment," Syndicated, 1995

James Ellroy's L. A. City of Demons, "The Scandal Rags," Investigation Discovery Channel, January 26, 2011

"Murder in Hollywood: A Tale of Vice and Vixens," History Channel

"Murder in Scottsdale, Special Feature Auto Focus," DVD, 2002

Now it Can Be Told, Geraldo Rivera (Host), "George Reeves," Cable News Network, 1992

BIBLIOGRAPHY

Now it Can Be Told, Geraldo Rivera (Host), "Marti Rulli and Dennis Davern," Cable News Network, 1992

Piers Morgan Tonight, "Robert Blake," Cable News Network, July 11, 2012

Rogue's Gallery, Mickey Cohen, Andrew Solt Productions, 1998

Talk of The Town, John Craig, Long Beach, California, Public Access, 1992

The Cat's Meow, Lion's Gate, DVD Release September 9, 2003

The Late, Late Show, Tom Snyder (Host), CBS, "Robert Blake", 1996.

A Note about the Photographs

Many of the photographs in this book are publicity pictures from various films and television shows that are being used under "Fair Editorial Use" 17 USC § 107. These are posed publicity photos and not stills. The purpose of these photos is to create interest in the pictured television programs and films. These films are not playing at your local Cineplex (although they should be), and the TV programs are no longer on network television.

The best way to fulfill the primary intended purpose of these photographs for publicity is to let you know that the following films or television shows are available on DVD or BluRay at Amazon, Barnes and Noble, or other retailers.

This book is also a historical work detailing biographies of notable and notorious persons, cinematic history, and historical incidents of true crime; therefore, it is educational. Editorial images used in this work illustrate this history and are being used for educational purposes.

Red Dust (1932)—Warner Archive, ASIN: B009RNK10K

Monkey Business (1931)—Universal Studios, ASIN: B004P9UWLY

Man Hunt (1941)—20th Century Fox, ASIN: B001SMC9L2

The Postman Always Rings Twice (1946)—Warner Home Video,

ASIN: B008PJZE0E

Johnny Eager (1942)—MGM, ASIN: B002ANUN4S

Adventures of Superman—The Complete First Six Seasons, Warner Home
Video, ASIN: B000HWZ4GQ

So Proudly We Hail (1943)—Universal Studios, ASIN: B000N3T0FU

Hogan's Heroes: The Komplete Series, Kommandant's Kollection (2010)—
Paramount, ASIN: B002L9N4O2

Police Woman - The Complete First Season (1974)—Sony Pictures Home
Entertainment - ASIN: B000E1EHPY

Gibbsville (1974)—(Not available on DVD as of this writing).

Tell it to the Judge (1949) SPE—ASIN: B00579FVYE

Teacher's Pet (1958)—Paramount, ASIN: B0007TKGY4

Come Fill The Cup (1951) (not available on DVD as of this writing; however, look for this excellent film on Turner Classic Movies, TCM)

They Shoot Horses Don't They—MGM Video and DVD - ASIN:
B0002KPHZQ

Miracle on 34th Street (1947)—20th Century Fox, ASIN: B000HT3PPG

Rebel Without a Cause (1955)—Warner Home Video - ASIN: B004GJYRAU

Splendor in the Grass (1961)—Warner Home Video - ASIN: B001LPWGGY

Bob and Carol and Ted and Alice (1969)—Image Entertainment - ASIN: B00441GYR4

Mokey (1942) (Not available on DVD as of this writing; however, look for it on Turner Classic Movies, TCM)

In Cold Blood (1967)—Sony Pictures Home Entertainment - ASIN: B003TNVZR2

This Property is Condemned (1966)—Paramount - ASIN: B0000AUHQA

A & E Biography DVDs of Jean Harlow, Bob Crane, George Reeves and Natalie Wood are available at http://shop.history.com/?v=biography

Index

About The Author

Dina Di Mambro is a film historian and entertainment writer who has worked as a research consultant for A & E Biography and "E" Entertainment Television. As a journalist, she has interviewed such luminaries as Glenn Ford, Shirley MacLaine, and Dyan Cannon.

As Dina-Marie Kulzer, she authored *Television Series Regulars of the Fifties and Sixties in Interview,* McFarland Publishers, © 1992, 2012 that consists of twenty-two interviews with Ralph Bellamy, Angela Cartwright, Barbara Eden, Kathy Garver, Gale Gordon, Don Grady, Linda Kaye Henning, Anne Jeffreys, Meredith MacRae, Julie Newmar, Gary Owens, Paul Petersen, Kasey Rogers, Rose Marie, James Stacy, Connie Stevens, Deborah Walley, Ray Walston, Dawn Wells, Jane Wyatt, Dick York, and Alan Young. www.mcfarland.com

Dina Di Mambro lives in Southern California.

Made in the USA
Charleston, SC
23 December 2013